BK 973.82 H712C
CUSTER AND THE LITTLE BIG HORN : A
PSYCHOBIOGRAPHICAL INQUIRY /HOFLING,
1981 15.95 FP
3000 579007 20015
St. Louis Community College

D0072764

CUSTER AND THE LITTLE BIG HORN

CUSTER
and the
Little Big Horn

A Psychobiographical Inquiry

CHARLES K. HOFLING, M.D.

Saint Louis University

WAYNE STATE UNIVERSITY PRESS

Detroit, 1981

Library of Congress Cataloging in Publication Data

Hofling, Charles K
Custer and Little Big Horn.

Bibliography: p. 111
Includes index.

1. Little Big Horn, Battle of the, 1876. 2. Custer, George Armstrong, 1839–1876. 3. Generals—United States—Biography. 4. United States. Army. 7th Cavalry—Biography. I. Title.

E83.876.C983H63 973.8′2′0924 [B] 80–23312
ISBN 0–8143–1668–9

Grateful acknowledgment is made for permission to quote from the following: W. A. Graham, *The Custer Myth: A Source Book of Custeriana* (Harrisburg, Pa.: Stackpole Co., 1953); Marguerite Merington, ed., *The Custer Story* (New York: Devin-Adair, 1950), copyright renewed 1978, by permission of The Devin-Adair Co., Old Greenwich, Conn. 06870; Jay Monaghan, *Custer: The Life of General George Armstrong Custer* (Lincoln, Nebr.: University of Nebraska Press, 1971), copyright © 1959, by James Monaghan; Bruce Rosenberg, *Custer and the Epic of Defeat* (University Park, Pa.: Pennsylvania State University Press, 1974).

The photograph of Major Marcus A. Reno is reproduced by permission of the Smithsonian Institution, Washington, D.C. All other photographs are courtesy of the Custer Battlefield National Monument, National Park Service, Department of Interior.

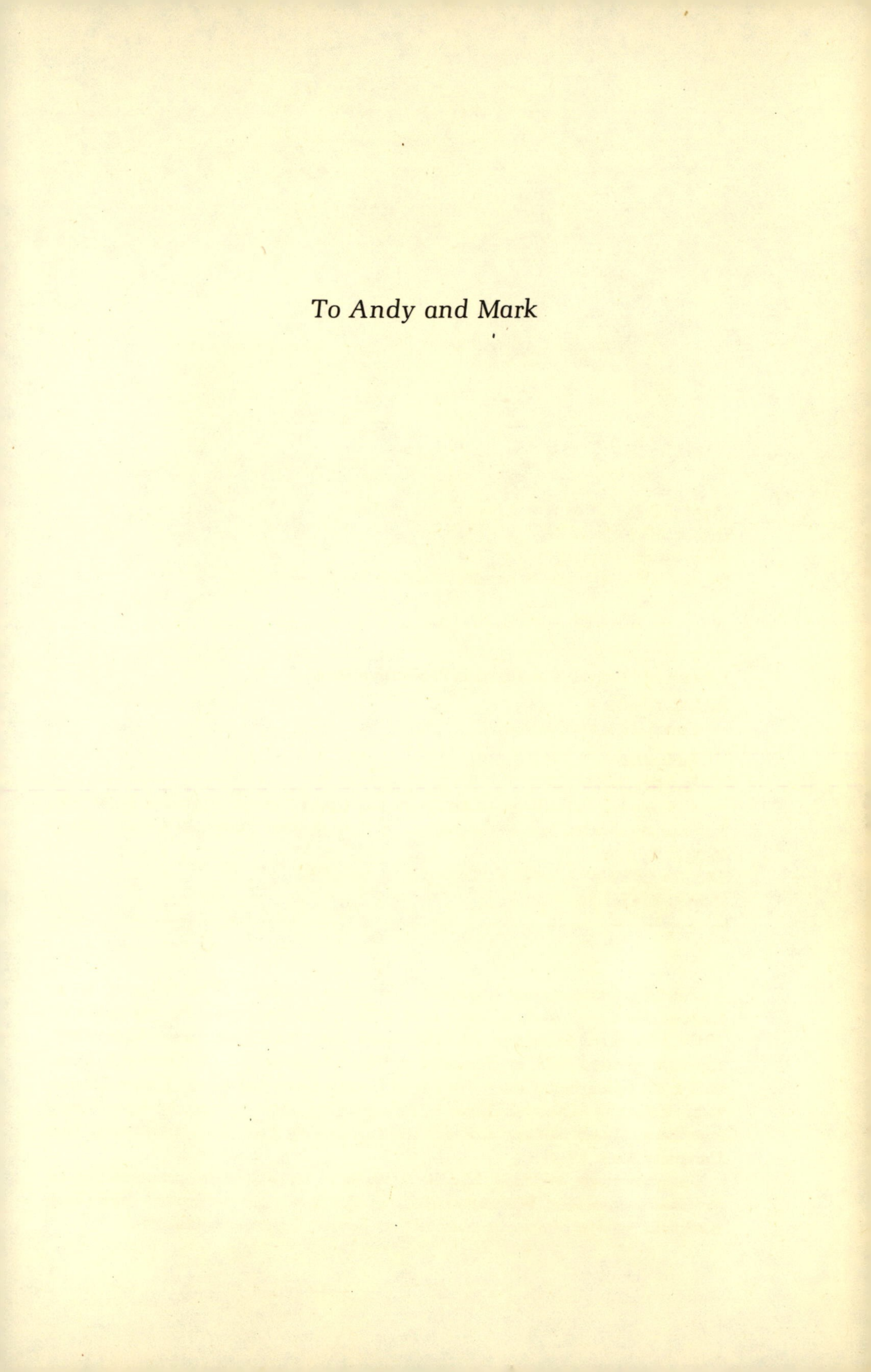

To Andy and Mark

Contents

MAPS AND ILLUSTRATIONS

Preface

My interest in General Custer and the Little Big Horn fight first stirred some twenty-five years ago. At that time, while I was in military service, I had as a patient a noncommissioned officer who was a Cheyenne and whose grandfather had participated in the battle. When I was on duty in the evening, and after we had gotten to know each other, he would sometimes tell me stories of the Plains Indians and especially of the battle which occurred at the Little Big Horn River.

This contact was of lasting value to me, for it opened my eyes to a realization of the evils of this country's Indian policies. (Perhaps it was of value to my patient also; at least, he recovered.) As the battle story unfolded, Custer and the Seventh Cavalry were, for the most part, mere foils for the feats of the Cheyenne heroes and their Sioux allies, but there was one exception to this: it appeared as my patient indicated very clearly the special, almost unique place which this encounter occupied in history. In the long story of Indian disappointments, occasional successes, but repeated defeats at the hands of the whites, there was at least this occasion on which they met an elite foe and won a dramatic victory. My Cheyenne friend emphasized that his ancestors and their Sioux allies had been up against a first-class fighting outfit, led by a celebrated commander (although they had mistaken his identity at the time). There was thus a lingering paradox in my mind: how was it that the most signal victory of the Sioux and Cheyenne was accomplished against what was supposed to be their most effective opponent?

Perhaps ten years later, one of my sons acquired one of the lithographs made from Otto Becker's 1895 painting *Custer's Last Fight*. This painting, commissioned by Anheuser-Busch, is the most famous portrayal of the battle; lithographs made from it at one time hung in thousands of saloons across the country. The picture shows Custer with upraised saber in his right hand and revolver in the other, standing in the midst of a few dying troopers and about to be overwhelmed by Indians moving in from all directions. "How did it happen?" asked the boy. I didn't really know, so we began to look into it. As we did, the paradox recurred to mind, but I soon perceived it in different terms. There was really no mystery as to why the Indians, given the conditions of 25 June 1876, had inflicted a crushing defeat on Custer and the Seventh Cavalry. The Sioux and Cheyenne were numerous; they were valiant and determined; they were reasonably well armed; and they were well led. Yet there is a difference between defeat and near-annihilation. There were, as one began to study the matter, certain questions about George Armstrong Custer: questions as to why he went into battle under the conditions which existed, why he brought on the battle at just the time he did, why he used just the tactics he did.

Questions such as these—as any student of the Indian Wars would have known—had been debated ever since the Little Big Horn fight. Many of them were answered, at least in part, but the material seemed incomplete with respect to Custer's personality and motives. There were, it seemed, certain clues. For example, on reading Col. W. A. Graham's *Story of the Little Big Horn,* I was struck by the highly dubious wisdom of Custer's ordering Captain Benteen on the famous "scout to the left" just before moving the rest of the command into the valley in which the Indian village was supposed to lie. It occurred to me that this action, which seriously weakened the attacking force, could best be understood if it were considered to be a *gesture* on Custer's part, a gesture of compliance with General Terry's wishes, which Custer had thus far not hesitated to ignore.[1] It was a very costly gesture and one seemingly not in accord with the frame of mind of a battle-wise commander intent on producing victory. It appeared to point to an ambivalence on Custer's part toward Terry, and such an ambivalence could have seriously compromised Custer's effectiveness in his mission.

A second clue came from reading F. W. Van de Water's *Glory-Hunter.* Beautifully written, the book seemed to me nevertheless simplistic as well as biased in its attempt to reduce the understanding of Custer's personality and life to a single motive, his vaunting ambition. By its reductionistic exaggeration, the work strongly inclined me as a psychiatrist to look for counter-motives, presumably unconscious, in an attempt to account for the ups and downs in Custer's career. It seemed, on further consideration, that a workable hypothesis might be that there were in Custer conscience factors (largely unconscious) which interacted with the ambitious strivings, producing the cyclic pattern. That this sort of psychological situation occurs frequently and can be productive of profound results was shown long ago by a number of psychoanalysts, notably Franz Alexander.[2]

Around these two clues and a handful of related ideas, I composed a thesis which appeared in the form of an essay, "General Custer and the Battle of the Little Big Horn."[3] This was largely an intuitive study, however, and further research as well as letters from readers soon convinced me that the formulations were both incomplete and in need of more documentation. The present work is the result of extensive further efforts to get at the facts of Custer's personal life and of his conduct of the Little Big Horn fight and to develop a well-rounded picture of the way his personality may have affected his actions at this most critical point.

Obtaining the factual material for the study proved an interesting task. One of my sons and I spent a good bit of time going over the Custer Battlefield with binoculars, compass, and pedometer. The basic terrain is largely unchanged. In any other than the tourist season it is a lonely spot; it is, as Charles Kuhlman has said, "a place where the ghosts walk in broad daylight."[4] On a more prosaic level, the Custer Battlefield Museum offers a wealth of information about Custer, his family, the Seventh Cavalry, the Indians, and the circumstances of the battle.[5]

An equally interesting experience in my quest for information was a visit to Monroe, Michigan, long the home of the Custer family, and to Dr. Lawrence A. Frost, its former mayor and perhaps the world's best-informed Custer scholar. Frost's collection of letters and telegrams sent to or by Custer and his wife Elizabeth and of books from Custer's library may well be unequaled; certainly it would be difficult to equal the courtesy with which he made available this material.

Library research was, of course, an essential part of the information-seeking. Among the more valuable sources of original material I consulted are the Custer Collection of the Monroe County Historical Museum Library; the Billings, Montana, Public Library; the Library of Eastern Montana State University (Billings), housing the Elizabeth B. Custer Collection; the National Archives; the Library of Congress; and the Yale University Library.

A brief comment may be in order regarding the readers for whom this volume is intended, insofar as their widely differing backgrounds have affected the selection of the material presented. For the potential readers whose historical interest is general, not specific to the Old West, and for those whose interest is primarily in applied psychoanalysis, I have considered it helpful, and even necessary, to include a great deal of factual material which is available elsewhere (though not all within a single cover). On the other hand, I am well aware that there is a sizable group of potential readers who are well versed in western history in general and in Seventh Cavalry matters in particular. I beg the indulgence of this group, who may prefer to concentrate on those chapters which present more intimate biographical details of Custer and the psychological implications of them.

After the manuscript had reached near final form, I called upon the assistance of various scholars in criticizing the contents from their respective points of view. Karl Menninger, M.D., and Robert G. Menninger, M.D., of the Menninger Foundation and Alvin Frank, M.D., of the Saint Louis Psychoanalytic Institute offered comments upon psychological and psychoanalytic matters. Walter J. Ong, S.J., Ph.D., of Saint Louis University did the same with respect to literary style and structure. Walter Consuelo Langsam, Ph.D., professor emeritus of history and president emeritus of the University of Cincinnati, reviewed the manuscript from the standpoints both of style and of general historical principles. Dr. Lawrence A. Frost reviewed chapters 2 through 9 from the standpoint of his special knowledge of Custer's career and the Custer family. John M. Carroll read the entire manuscript and offered encouraging comments. Jay Monaghan of the University of California, Santa Barbara, answered a number of specific questions of fact with respect to Custer's background. To all these gentlemen I am deeply grateful. Conjectures offered in this volume and errors which may remain in the presentation are, of course, my own.

Special thanks are due my wife, Madelyn L. Hofling, and my sons, Charles Andrew and Mark Laymon, for their assistance in various phases of the work. The industry and skill of my secretaries, Mrs. Rose Garibay and Mrs. Janice Stumpf, are deeply appreciated. The Saint Louis University Department of Psychiatry has given generous support to the undertaking. The Wayne State University Press and particularly my editor, Sherwyn T. Carr, have shown resourcefulness and offered sustained encouragement.

ONE

Introduction

THE Battle of the Little Big Horn and its enigmatic climax, Custer's Last Stand, have gripped the American imagination generation after generation. More has been written about the fight than about any other battle in American history, not excluding Gettysburg. A bibliography of magazine and journal articles alone fills a volume.[1] Motion pictures have reflected a similar degree of interest. The past thirty years have seen *They Died with Their Boots On, Custer's Last Stand, Sitting Bull, Tonka, 7th Cavalry, Custer of the West,* and *Little Big Man,* to name only a few. There have also been a number of television productions, including a fifteen-installment series called "Custer's Last Stand."

The Custer Battlefield National Monument, a national park at the site of the battle, attracts about 200,000 visitors annually, despite its location far from any major population center. Visitors have also come for many years to look at the three principal Custer monuments: at West Point; in Monroe, Michigan; and in New Rumley, Ohio. There is an organized group, the Little Big Horn Associates, devoted to a continuing study of the battle, its principal figures, and various related circumstances. Since 1974 this group has sponsored an annual series of seminars on the general subject.

Phenomena such as these constitute clear evidence of a continuing public interest. What is less clear is the nature of this interest.[2] For one thing, of course, the Battle of the Little Big Horn is of some significance as a quite conscious symbol. It was the most spectacular victory of red fighting men over white in American history, and yet it ushered in the beginning of the end of freedom for the Plains Indians. But obviously it means more: the unflagging interest of military scholars, of students of the Old West, and, to a lesser degree, of the general public is by no means confined to the battle as a symbol; it is invested in its detail as fact.[3] This circumstance suggests that the really important symbolism is not fully conscious. It is perhaps analogous to that which brings viewers back again and again—often with quite mixed emotions—to view a celebrated painting or play.

Most historically remembered battles tend to become sources of controversy. This is true, for example, of Waterloo, of the first Battle of the Marne, of the Battle of the Bulge, and certainly of Gettysburg, and it was, from the very first, exceptionally true of the Battle of the Little Big Horn. The grounds of the controversy have shifted greatly from time to time, but the controversy has continued almost as if it had a life of its own. The campaign against the Indians, of which the Battle of the Little Big Horn was the most striking feature, had political and ideological implications from the first, and this circumstance stimulated controversy.[4] After a long period of political exile, the Democratic party was eager to regain control of the White House, and the scandals of Ulysses S. Grant's administration made this hope seem well within reach. The defeat of the Seventh Cavalry, with the annihilation of the five troops under Custer's personal command, was excellent propaganda material. Grant's Peace Policy toward the Indians had been widely considered, particularly in the West and South, as being too conciliatory, and it was now heavily assailed in much of the press. It was maintained that the army was undermanned and inadequately equipped and that traders had been permitted to sell more efficient firearms to the Indians than were available to the soldiers.

There was naturally a hunt for a scapegoat to blame for the military reverse. At first the principal candidates were Custer and his immediate superior, Gen. Alfred Terry. Both were well known, Custer by reason of his colorful career and personality and Terry because he held the important position of commanding general of the Department of Dakota. The controversy over which of the two to blame was given immediate impetus by an unfortunate circumstance. Terry wrote two reports of the battle within ten days of its occurrence. The first, composed on the battlefield on 27 June, was a purely factual, dry account of events as they had transpired. By implication, Terry shouldered whatever blame might be attached to the military failure. This report was given to a scout, Muggins Taylor, to carry to Fort Ellis on the Gallatin River in Montana Territory, where it was to be telegraphed to Salt Lake City and thence to Chicago, the headquarters of Gen. Philip Sheridan. As luck would have it, the telegraph wires were down somewhere between Fort Ellis and Salt Lake City, and the message was delayed.

Meanwhile, on 2 July, at the confluence of the Big Horn and Yellowstone rivers, Terry wrote a second, confidential report to Sheridan and to Gen. William Tecumseh Sherman, the chief of staff, in which he outlined his plan of battle, noted that it had been disregarded by Custer, and said, "I feel that our plan must have been successful it if had been carried out."[5] This report was carried by one of Terry's staff officers, Capt. Edward W. Smith, to Bismarck, North Dakota, and then telegraphed to Chicago. It reached Chicago on 6 July. Both Sheridan and Sherman were in Philadelphia to attend the Centennial Exposition, and the message was relayed to them without mishap. Sherman, however, wishing Secretary of War James D. Cameron to see it without delay, gave it to a man who was posing as an official messenger, but who was in fact a reporter for the *Philadelphia Enquirer*. Seeing that he had the scoop of the decade, the reporter wrote up the news for his paper, and it appeared in most big-city papers on 7 July. It was not until the following day that the first report, intended for general consumption, reached Washington, and it did not appear in the press until 9 July. The publication of the confidential report and the sequence in which the reports reached the public gave the impression that Terry was trying to make a scapegoat of Custer, placing all the blame upon a dead man. While Terry's second report was somewhat defensive, this impression was far from the truth. Terry never responded publicly to the criticism on this score (though he was hurt by it), but others did, and a serious dispute over responsibility developed which has continued to the present time.[6]

Shortly after the battle, another question arose in conversations and in print: had Custer's principal subordinates, Maj. Marcus A. Reno and Capt. Frederick Benteen, betrayed their commander by not performing adequately in the battle? Reno, as the second in command, had to bear the brunt of the criticism. This controversy became intense at the end of 1876, when Frederick Whittaker, a novelist and an ardent admirer of Custer, published his *Complete Life of Gen. George A. Custer*—much publicized and widely read—in which he placed the blame for the defeat squarely upon Reno's shoulders, accusing the major of cowardice and disobedience. Editorials and letters to the editor appeared in many papers, taking both sides of the question, but for the most part casting aspersions on Reno. Finally, in 1878, Reno requested that a military court of inquiry be convened to look into the question of his conduct at the Battle of the Little Big Horn. This was done, and the court met in Chicago at the old Palmer House from 13 January to 12 February 1879. It concluded: "The conduct of the officers throughout was excellent and while subordinates in some instances did more for the safety of the command than did Major Reno, there was nothing in his conduct which requires animadversion from this Court."[7] This conclusion was damning with faint praise. While the proceedings of the court have formed a valuable source for historians of the battle, they did not fully dispel the cloud hanging over Reno. His behavior was becoming erratic and indiscreet. Details are largely based on hearsay, but he was said to be drinking more than was good for him, and, following a court-martial, he was dismissed from the army on 1 April 1880.[8]

Arguments about the battle continued, involving questions of strategy and tactics as well as the personalities of the leading figures among the whites. With the passing of time, various officers and men involved wrote articles about the fight, and in the 1890s there was a spirited argument in print between Col. Edward S. Godfrey (present at the battle) and Gen. James B. Fry, on the one hand, and Col. Robert P. Hughes (Terry's aide), on the other, as to whether or not Custer had disobeyed orders. At about this time the Indian versions of the story also began to appear, but these varied widely among themselves and for a long time only added to the controversy.

Whittaker's 1876 biography was clearly that of a Custer partisan and, though utilizing contemporary sources, contained numerous inaccuracies. Its counterweight for the general public was Frederick Van de Water's *Glory-Hunter* (1934), a condemnatory biography written in the naively psychological style of Emil Ludwig and containing a number of inaccuracies of its own. Col. W. A. Graham's *Story of the Little Big Horn* (1926; 1941) took a neutral attitude toward the military figures involved in the battle, but sought to protect the army's reputation and that of the Seventh Cavalry. In recent years a number of more evenhanded studies have appeared, including Jay Monaghan's biography, *Custer* (1959); Edgar I. Stewart's *Custer's Luck* (1955), a detailed account of the battle itself and the campaign of 1876; and John S. Gray's splendidly researched *Sioux War of 1876* (1976). Controversy still is acute, however, although now with less regard to personality and more to ideology. Not surprisingly, in view of his fame and flamboyance, Custer has come to represent a policy of which he was but one of many instruments and a point of view with which he was at times in disagreement. The result is that the real person has become obscured. Just as Custer was portrayed for a long time as a sort of stage hero, now (as in the film *Little Big Man* or Mari Sandoz's *Battle of the Little Bighorn* [1966]), he is usually represented as a stage villain. The real man, with his strengths and weaknesses, doubts and impulses, conflicts and defenses, tends to be grossly distorted.

Clearly there is the stuff of legends in the story of the Little Big Horn. If the Plains Indians had been able to resist the advance of the whites and had maintained a cohesive civilization of their own, it seems likely that the Little Big Horn fight would have been the subject of an orally transmitted epic and eventually of a written one. It might have become the *Iliad* of an Indian Homer. As it is, there has been something very like an epic development of the story among whites. Longfellow, Whittier, and many other poets have written about Custer and the Little Big Horn; Walt Whitman's "From Far Dakota's Canyons" in particular is an excellent poem.

Bruce Rosenberg has pointed out how closely the ingredients of the Custer–Little Big Horn story parallel those of the classic epics of various cultures. Making special reference to the French *Chanson de Roland* and the English *Morte Arthure*, he describes the archetypal (that is, stylized, not necessarily historical) situation.

> The losers who interest us are not pathetic—they are magnificent, for they lose with memorable dignity and *elan*. An aura of sublime glory gathers about their names and deeds. . . . Defeat itself becomes the medium by which the majesty of these vanquished is manifested. . . .
>
> Thus we are interested in the most distinctive of heroes, members of a special club. Each is a hero who has only a small army with him, and though they fight on with great tenacity, they are eventually worn down by the copious numbers ranged against them. . . . their enemy are racial (or national) aliens sworn to destroy the hero's people.
>
> As the one-sided battle grinds on, the hero and his men know what the outcome must inevitably be. Their situation is hopeless, further fighting is useless, yet because he is the man he is, and they are the loyal followers they are, they steel themselves to make the enemy pay dearly for each of their lives. In the last few minutes of life left to them, the hero and a few survivors, weary yet determined as ever, withdraw to a hilltop to make their final stand. And it is here, when all of his men have been cut down, that their commander wrings out the last ounce of retaliation against his inexorable foe.
>
> But not everyone has died on that hilltop: one man, an unimportant spear carrier who stands inconspicuously near the wings of the spectacular grand finale, makes his escape from the carnage and carries the tale to the waiting world. This lone survivor will shortly be

forgotten, but his story will outlive him, and it is his story which rouses his countrymen to a fury of vengeful energy, and with the memory of their fallen hero alive in their hearts they drive the barbarians away in terror and confusion. Then, when the dust has settled, they realize that not even the great multitude of the enemy could strike their hero down had he not been betrayed.[9]

It is indeed striking to observe how closely the story of Custer's Last Stand, as portrayed by Whittaker and other romantic writers, parallels this archetypal story. Since America was already in the grip of the printed word, no true oral epic could result, but the similarities of the romanticized story to the features of such epics go far to explain the hold it has had upon the popular imagination. Moreover, it is these very elements (heroic and romantic on a large scale) which recently, in the day of the antihero, have lent themselves to a process of exposure and inversion which makes of Custer an archvillain instead of an archhero. His reputation has suffered in the twentieth century as a result of a general cultural disillusionment with and reaction against the very qualities for which he was praised in the nineteenth. At least since World War I, many intellectuals have seemed to feel it almost their duty to deprecate physical courage and naive patriotism and to seek flaws in those individuals who embody them.

Any attempt to write a historical essay about Custer and the Battle of the Little Big Horn today, more than one hundred years after the event, is fraught with serious difficulties. All the figures involved are gone, although some died more recently than might be generally supposed. Lt. Charles Varnum, chief of Custer's scouts, died in 1935, Custer's widow Elizabeth in 1933. The last white survivor of the battle, Sgt. Charles Windolph, died in 1950. Some of the Indian warriors were very young at the time of the battle, perhaps not more than twelve, and some of these survived all the whites. Much has remained in the way of written reports and correspondence, both semipublic and private, though this material is often biased and must be used with care.

All things considered, however, the advantages of writing and analyzing the story many years later considerably outweigh the disadvantages. For one thing, the heat of controversy has generated a wealth of studies of a technical, military nature, concerning themselves with an hour-by-hour—and, at certain points, almost a minute-by-minute—account of events in the actual battle. Although these accounts sometimes conflict, many were based upon the discovery of details which must be regarded as factual, and, in considering a great number of these accounts, one finds that the inconsistencies tend often to be eliminated by a preponderance of evidence. Then too, the whole Custer family—and particularly Custer and Elizabeth—were voluminous correspondents, and much of their writing, which, whatever its biases, does reflect the thoughts and emotions of the individual writing at the time, has been preserved. Perhaps most important is the matter of perspective. With the distancing of more than a hundred years, a considerable degree of objectivity becomes possible. Moreover, the Battle of the Little Big Horn and

Custer's actions in it, despite their intrinsic interest and their symbolic significance, can be seen as small events. That is to say, American history presumably would not have turned out very differently if the whites had won the fight or if it had never happened.

To one attempting to construct a scientific analysis, especially one which includes a study of motives, there is an immense advantage in all this. It is a corollary of human nature that, the larger and more recent an event, the greater will be the ideological and personal biases in the would-be historian. To do a scientific job, he must be interested in his subject matter, but it is equally important that he be very largely free (to be completely free would be an impossibility) of personal involvement. He must not care very much, *personally,* about the way things turned out at the time in question and be free to concentrate on *just how it was* that they turned out the way they did.[10]

The scope and focus of the present study should be made clear. It is not a comprehensive biography of George Armstrong Custer, nor is it a comprehensive account of the campaign of 1876 against the Sioux and Northern Cheyenne. It is an intensive study of the Battle of the Little Big Horn. Certain widely accepted inferences regarding the existing conditions and the actions of the leading figures will be questioned. In particular, it is a study which raises key questions about Custer's behavior, including his decisions and the motivations for them, which have not been completely answered by earlier works. These questions lead to a study of Custer the man—what his personality was like, how it developed as it did, and how it affected his actions just before and during the Little Big Horn fight. This effort necessarily involves a good bit of speculation. This is a psychobiography of Custer, and speculation is unavoidable. What is promised, however, is an effort to indicate clearly what is fact and what is speculation, and to use only such speculation as represents the balance of probability and is internally consistent.

TWO

Background to the Campaign of 1876

DURING most of the Civil War there was a period of relative quiet in the long struggle between the Indians of the northern plains and the westward-moving settlers from the United States. This very fact is a strong indication that the Plains Indians wanted nothing so much as to be permitted to go their own way. There were, however, some incidents of violence. In late 1864, for example, Col. John M. Chivington, under pressure from white settlers, made an attack on a Cheyenne village lying within a Cheyenne and Arapahoe reservation at Sand Creek, Colorado. In much of the eastern press the incident was referred to as "the Chivington massacre." As Edgar Stewart has said, "Whether it was a justifiable attack on a hostile village that was masquerading as peaceful in order to escape punishment, or the wanton massacre of peaceful tribesmen, probably never will be known."[1] The Indians retaliated, however, and during the latter half of the 1860s the pressure on them mounted as ranchers, farmers, and miners moved west from the Missouri River and east from California and the Oregon Territory. The Bozeman Trail, leading to the gold fields in southern Montana (discovered in 1861) was fortified. Construction of the Union Pacific Railroad was speeded up. Clashes between Indians and whites multiplied. The Indians realized that the inroads of the whites, with the large-scale destruction of game, would soon mean an end to their way of life. Irregular but fairly intensive warfare developed between the Sioux and their allies, the Northern Cheyenne, and the United States. Throughout 1866 and 1867 the Indians, with Red Cloud of the Cheyenne and Sitting Bull of the Sioux as their principal chiefs, held their own.

A peace commission from Washington went to the plains in late 1867, and in 1868 a treaty was signed at Fort Laramie, Wyoming Territory, with a number of representative chiefs led by Red Cloud. This treaty appeared to signal a clear victory for the Indians. Its principal provisions were as follows: (1) war between the United States and the treaty Indians was prohibited; (2) the Sioux Nation was given as a permanent reservation all of what is now South Dakota lying west of the Missouri River, including the sacred Black Hills country; (3) that portion of what is now Wyoming and Montana lying north of the Platte River and east of the summit of the Big Horn Mountains was to be considered "unceded Indian territory" and not to be entered by the whites without Indian consent; (4) the Sioux were to permit the construction of the Union Pacific Railroad and any future railroads "not passing through their reservation"; and (5) the forts on the Bozeman Trail were to be abandoned.[2] Although Red Cloud's prestige was great at this time, a number of the Plains Indians leaders, Sitting Bull among them, believed that the word of the white man could not be trusted. They therefore neither signed the treaty nor settled on the South Dakota reservation.

As might have been predicted, the treaty was not long maintained. Violations were committed on both sides, and for somewhat the same reason: neither the government of the United States nor Red Cloud and the other treaty chiefs could enforce its provisions properly. It seems clear, however, that the more numerous, athough not necessarily the deadlier, violations were made by the whites. The railroads could not long be held back, and their advance meant laying tracks over the "unceded territory." Gold was found in the Black Hills by an expedition of questionable legality, and the prospectors who rushed in could not be stopped.[3] The government tried to purchase a part of the Yellowstone River country from the Sioux and Cheyenne, but this attempt failed. At the same time, Indian depredations upon white settlers in areas of Nebraska, Minnesota, Wyoming, and Montana, areas lying outside of Indian territory, were assuming serious proportions. These attacks were perhaps made chiefly by the nonreservation, nontreaty Indians (the so-called hostiles), but the distinction between the two groups was never clear, for it was the custom of many young braves whose chiefs had signed the treaty of 1868 to leave the reservations in the summer and share the life and warlike activity of the nontreaty Indians.

A final effort was made by Commissioner of Indian Affairs E. C. Smith to avoid large-scale bloodshed. In the early winter of 1875–76, word was sent to all the nonreservation Sioux and Northern Cheyenne to come in and settle on the reservations or else face punitive expeditions. The deadline for settlement was 31 January 1876. By this date few of the hostiles had responded and almost none had complied. (Very likely some had not been reached by the messengers.) Accordingly the project of "disciplining and bringing in the recalcitrant Sioux and Cheyenne" was turned over to the War Department.[4]

At this time William T. Sherman was army chief of staff under President Ulysses S. Grant. The army was organized into three major commands: the Division of the Atlantic, the Division of the Pacific, and the Division of the Missouri. The Division of the Missouri, which included all the Plains area from Canada to the Gulf of Mexico, was under the command of Lt. Gen. Philip Sheridan, with headquarters in Chicago. It consisted of four departments, of which two, the Department of the Platte under Brig. Gen. George Crook (with headquarters in Omaha) and the Department of Dakota under Brig. Gen. Alfred H. Terry (with headquarters in Saint Paul), were to be involved in the campaign against the Sioux and Northern Cheyenne.

Sheridan's general plan involved moving three columns of soldiers into the territory of the hostiles—the large area called "unceded territory" in the treaty of 1868. One of these was to move east from Montana, one west from North Dakota, and one north from the Platte River. Thus the northern, eastern, and southern boundaries of the territory to be invaded would be crossed (and, as it was rather naively thought, covered) by the advancing columns. The western boundary, marked by the peaks of the Big Horn Mountains, would be ignored, a decision that was considered workable since the area to the west was the home of the Crow Nation, which was both the hereditary enemy of the Sioux and informally allied with the whites because of reasonably good relations with the old-time "mountain men."

The column which moved up from the south was under the command of General Crook, and its activities, while of considerable importance in the context of the entire campaign, affected the Battle of the Little Big Horn only indirectly. On 17 June 1876, Crook's column was defeated, or at least stopped in its advance, by Sioux warriors, probably under the leadership of Crazy Horse. This success filled the Indians with confidence and made them readier to make a stand at the Little Big Horn than might otherwise have been the case. The other two columns were commanded by General Terry. The one moving east from Montana was headed by Col. John Gibbon and consisted of six companies of infantry and a battalion (four companies) of the Second Cavalry under Maj. James Brisbin, about 345 men in all, with a Napoleon gun and two Gatling guns. Gibbon's orders were to patrol the Yellowstone River, making certain that the hostile Indians did not cross it and move north, and, if possible, to locate their principal camp or camps south of the river before rendezvousing with the Dakota column. Gibbon's contingent performed both of its assigned tasks adequately, but it did not do any fighting, nor did Gibbon speed on to Terry the news that a sizable Indian village had in fact been found south of the Yellowstone.[5]

The Dakota column was quartered in and around Fort Abraham Lincoln, North Dakota. Sheridan originally planned for it to be commanded by Lt. Col. (Brt. Maj. Gen.) George Armstrong Custer, and it was to have begun its advance in early spring. Neither of these arrangements was carried out because of a highly unusual set of circumstances in part provoked by the commander-designate.

Among the various scandals of the Grant administration, the one most conspicuous to army personnel, and particularly to those quartered on the frontier, was the mismanagement of army post traderships. The traders, replacing the sutlers of Civil War days, were appointed by the secretary of war and licensed to sell or trade goods—without competition—on military and Indian reservations. At posts which were near cities, the high prices and poor quality that were often characteristic of the traders' goods were merely an inconvenience, but at frontier posts they often became a serious evil. Moreover, since traderships produced a high income, they were much sought after, and the appointments were often sold by Grant's secretary of war, W. W. Belknap. Although it was illegal for one man to operate more than a single tradership, this restriction was often violated. Among the violaters was the president's brother, Orvil Grant.

Custer, as commandant of Fort Lincoln, was fully aware of the hardships to his men, and he became convinced of the illegalities of the operation through gossip which was circulating freely about the area. While visiting in the East in the winter of 1875–76, he had been outspokenly critical of the situation. In February the Democratic House of Representatives set up a committee chaired by Democratic Representative Heister Clymer of Pennsylvania to investigate the scandal. Clymer was aware of Custer's remarks and summoned him to Washington to testify. Custer reached Washington on 26 March, remaining there until 2 May. (Secretary Belknap had resigned on 2 March, but since the Supreme Court had not ruled that impeachment could not take place after a resignation, the latter proceeding followed immediately on the committee hearings and continued for some time.) Custer's testimony received wide publicity, although most of it probably would not have been admissable at a trial, being largely hearsay. Among other matters, he testified that he had met Orvil Grant and a partner on a train going from Saint Paul to Bismarck, North Dakota, and that Grant had indicated that they were going to take possession of a number of trading posts. He also stated his opinion that an extension of the principal Sioux reservation to include the east bank of the Missouri River, ordered by the president, was designed primarily to increase the profits of certain traderships by giving them a monopoly.

The actual impeachment proceedings got under way on 17 April. Custer had hoped that once the Clymer hearings were over he would be permitted to return to Fort Lincoln, and on 20 April he telegraphed Terry that he was on the point of leaving Washington for Saint Paul. However, the impeachment managers asked him to repeat portions of his testimony before the full House of Representatives. Custer asked Terry to request that he be excused from this summons so that he might rejoin the command, which was being assembled at Fort Lincoln. Terry did so, but by then the matter was out of his hands. President Grant, incensed by Custer's testimony before the Clymer Committee, ordered the new secretary of war, J. D. Cameron, not to forward the request (which had gone through proper military channels and had been endorsed) to the impeachment managers. Grant also gave orders, through Sherman and Sheridan, to Terry that Custer was not to be in command of the expedition in the field. Terry was asked to suggest other possible commanders, but it must have seemed clear to army headquarters that the officers suggested were not as competent as Custer, for Terry was finally directed to assume direct command of the expedition himself.[6]

Custer had some idea of what was going on and that his career was in serious jeopardy. He eventually received permission from the impeachment managers to leave Washington. He was, however, unable to move without proper military orders, and since at this point he perceived that his destiny was being directed from the highest quarters, he called repeatedly at the White House, requesting an interview with the president. Grant would not see him and on one occasion kept him cooling his heels in an anteroom for an entire day. Custer sent him the following letter.

Washington, D.C.
May 1, 1876

To His Excellency
The President—

Today for the third time I have sought an interview with the President, not to solicit a favor—except to be granted a brief hearing, but to remove from his mind certain unjust impressions concerning myself which I have reason to believe are entertained against me. I desired this opportunity simply as a matter of justice, and I regret that the President has declined to give an opportunity to submit to him a brief statement which justice to him as well as to me demanded.

Respectfully submitted,

G. A. Custer
Lt. Col. 7th Cavalry
Bt. Major Gen'l., U. S. Army[7]

His letter was given no reply.

Custer, now desperate to return to Fort Lincoln, applied for and received permission from both the adjutant general and the inspector general of the army to leave Washington—whether these officers did not know what was going on or whether they were acting under secret instructions is not known—and he left for the West on 2 May. His departure gave Grant an opportunity for further harrassment, and on 3 May Custer was placed under arrest while his train was in Chicago. He telegraphed General Sherman for permission to proceed to Fort Lincoln. This was granted.[8]

On 5 May Sheridan's adjutant, Col. R. C. Drum, sent a telegram to Terry.

The Lieutenant General directs me to transmit for your information and guidance the following telegram from the General of the Army:

"Have just come from the President who orders that General Custer be allowed to rejoin his post, to remain there on duty, but not to accompany the expedition supposed to be on the point of starting against the hostile Indians under General Terry."
(signed) "W. T. Sherman"

R. C. Drum[9]

Thus within a short time Custer had lost command, not only of the entire expedition of the Department of the Missouri, but of his own regiment. His distress was overwhelming. He went to Terry's headquarters in Saint Paul, got down on his knees, and with tears in his eyes begged Terry's help. It was not withheld. The following message, of which every word, even those over Custer's signature (it is said on the authority of Col. Robert P. Hughes, Terry's aide) was of Terry's own composition, was sent to President Grant.

Headquarters, Department of Dakota
Saint Paul, Minn., May 6, 1876

Adjutant General,
Division Missouri,
Chicago

I forward the following:
To His excellency
The President,
through Military Channels,

I have seen your order, transmitted through the General of the Army, directing that I be not permitted to accompany the expedition about to move against the hostile Indians. As my entire regiment forms a part of the expedition and as I am the senior officer of the regiment on duty in this Department, I respectfully but most earnestly request that while not allowed to go in command of the expedition, I may be permitted to serve with my regiment in the field. I appeal to you as a soldier to spare me the humiliation of seeing my regiment march to meet the enemy and I not to share its dangers.

(Signed) G. A. Custer

In forwarding the above, I wish to say, expressly, that I have no desire whatever to question the orders of the President, or of any of my military superiors. Whether Lieutenant Colonel Custer shall be permitted to accompany my column or not, I shall go in command of it. I do not know the reasons upon which the orders already given rest; but if those reasons do not forbid it, Lieutenant Colonel Custer's services would be very valuable with his regiment.

(Signed) Terry
Commanding Department

A true Copy
Geo. T. Ruggles
Assistant Adjutant General[10]

Sheridan forwarded the letter as requested, adding an endorsement: "I am sorry Lieutenant Colonel Custer did not manifest as much interest in staying at his post to organize and get ready his regiment and the expedition as he now does to accompany it. On a previous occasion in eighteen sixty-eight I asked executive clemency for Colonel Custer to enable him to accompany his regiment against the Indians, and I sincerely hope that if granted this time it may have sufficient effect to prevent him from again attempting to throw discredit upon his profession and his brother officers.'' Grant relented and had the chief of staff, General Sherman, send word of this to Terry.

Headquarters of the Army
Washington, May 8th, 1876

To General A. H. Terry, St. Paul, Minn.:

General Sheridan's enclosing yours of yesterday touching General Custer's urgent request to go under your command with his regiment has been submitted to the President, who sent me word that if you want General Custer along he withdraws his objections. Advise Custer to be prudent, not to take along any newspaper men, who always make mischief, and to abstain from personalities in the future. . . .

W. T. Sherman,
General[11]

Upon receipt of this telegram, the final preparations for the departure of the Dakota column were made. During the last week of preparation, however, two curious incidents occurred, one in Saint Paul and one at Fort Abraham Lincoln. Within a matter of hours of learning of his partial reinstatement, Custer, who was still in Saint Paul, met an old friend at the Metropolitan Hotel, Col. William Ludlow of the Corps of Engineers. In speaking of the coming campaign, Custer told Ludlow that he felt certain that he could ''swing clear of Terry'' and be able to maneuver as he wished. Ludlow mentioned this startling conversation to several other officers that same day, and he intended to get word of it to Terry but did not succeed in doing so until after the campaign.

There must have been some reaction in Custer, however, for, as his wife wrote later to a friend:

A day before the expedition started, General Terry was in our house alone with Autie [Custer's pet name]. A's thoughts were calm, deliberate, and solemn. . . . I knew that he felt tenderly and affectionately toward [Terry]. On that day . . . he said very seriously . . . ''General Terry, a man usually means what he says when he brings his wife to listen to his statements. I want to say that reports are circulating that I do not want to go out on this campaign under you, but I want you to know that I do want to go and serve under you, not only that I value you as a soldier, but as a friend and a man.''[12]

It would almost certainly be a mistake to assume, as has sometimes been done, that Custer's remarks were solely a belated attempt at caution. They have the ring of sincerity, and they were taken by both Terry and Libbie Custer in that vein. One can only conclude that Custer's feelings about Terry and his leadership were highly ambivalent.

THREE

Preliminary Phases of Terry's Campaign

THE Seventh Cavalry was, in 1876 as later, a much publicized and celebrated regiment, having been in the public eye since the Battle of the Washita. Much has been made of the fact that it was not at full strength during the summer campaign against the Sioux and Cheyenne. Its twelve companies numbered only about 750 officers and men, and about 25 percent of the men had been with the regiment eight months or less.[1] These were not, however, unusual figures. In the post-Civil War years most units were not kept at full strength; since desertions were rather frequent, it was also not unusual to have a high percentage of relatively new enlistments. Furthermore—as was not unusual either—about half the new recruits to the Seventh had had previous military experience.[2] The campaign of 1876 was the first occasion on which all twelve companies of the regiment were assembled as a unit. Prior to this time several companies regularly had been on detached duty of one kind or another, but this had been the common lot of regiments both before and after the Civil War.

Probably a more serious matter was the shortage of officers. By the book there should, under combat conditions, have been forty-two officers: a colonel, a lieutenant colonel, and an adjutant at headquarters, a major for each of the three battalions, and thirty-six company officers, not counting three surgeons. As the regiment marched out on the expedition, it was without its colonel, two of its majors, four of its captains, and eight of its lieutenants.[3] There was also a shortage of seasoned noncommissioned officers, the exact extent of which is difficult to determine. These limitations, appreciable under any conditions, would be particularly serious if the regiment were thrown even temporarily on the defensive, since it would be difficult to exert control over the rate and manner of firing of the less experienced troopers.

Furthermore, the capabilities of the regiment were quite likely affected by factionalism among the officers. There has, no doubt, seldom been a fighting unit without some division of opinion as to the personality and merits of its commanding officer, but perhaps because of the smaller units and the more personalized leadership, such factionalism seems to have been especially characteristic of the "Old Army," the army in the period between the Civil War and World War I. There can be no question, however, but that Lt. Col. George Armstrong Custer was faced with it to an exceptional degree. Not only did he have a flamboyant personality, but he was appreciably younger than some of his senior subordinates. In spite of a good deal of mutual antagonism, he was forced to rely upon them.

At the beginning of the ill-fated expedition, Custer was, by reason of his exploits in the Civil War and on the frontier, one of the best-known officers in America. Only thirty-six years old, he was somewhat above average height, lean and sinewy, and blond, with a receding hairline and a drooping cavalry mustache. He was exceedingly fit, but years of outdoor living had given him a weather-beaten appearance, making him appear somewhat older than he was. His naturally fair complexion was almost continually sunburned and windburned when he was in the field. Ordinarily good-natured and fond of practical jokes, he was keen and intense and sometimes strove with difficulty to keep an even temper. His voice seems to have been rather high-pitched, especially under emotional stress, and at such times he occasionally stammered slightly. Undisciplined himself in his early years, he had become a strict disciplinarian. Seemingly devoid of physical fear, he was most effective when in combat. It has been said of the men in the ranks that, whatever they thought of Custer personally, they were always his admirers after having been led by him in battle.

The two ranking subordinates with the regiment at this time were the junior major, Marcus A. Reno, and the senior captain, Frederick W. Benteen. Both men were leaders of the anti-Custer faction. In neither case are the full sources of the interpersonal difficulties known, but certain elements are clear.

Reno was a West Pointer, having been graduated just before Custer entered. He had lingered on at the academy a few days and perhaps met Custer at that time. Reno was a dark, stocky, conventionally good-looking man. He was twice cited for bravery in the Civil War and had reached the rank of brigadier general of volunteers. He was thus used to important command and to privileges, and it was perhaps a stroke of ill fortune that had placed him in a position subordinate to a younger man, once five classes behind him, whose brilliant record outshone his own very good one. Unlike Custer and most of the company commanders, however, Reno had no experience at Indian fighting. Possibly because of the events at the Little Big Horn and their consequences, he was to come to a bad end. Although in 1877 he was formally exonerated of misconduct at the battle, Reno began to drink excessively and commit other indiscretions. He faced two courts-martial, and in April 1880 he was dismissed from the army for drunkenness and conduct unbecoming an officer (engaging in a tavern brawl).[4]

Benteen was a quite different sort. Indeed the two officers cared little for one another. They were linked primarily by their dislike of Custer—which, with Benteen, seems to have reached the level of hatred—and eventually by the necessity of defending their joint actions in the Battle of the Little Big Horn. Benteen was a year older than Reno and had a much stronger personality. Six years older than Custer, he was born into an aristocratic Virginia family, which moved in his youth to Missouri. Although his family owned slaves, Benteen was loyal to the Union, and he was commissioned at the outbreak of the war as a lieutenant in a regiment of Missouri volunteer cavalry. He rose in rank through every grade to that of colonel, primarily because of his outstanding combat leadership. Unlike Custer and most of the other officers, Benteen had an income besides his army pay; he seems not to have been ambitious and to have remained in the army primarily because he liked the life and found the work easy. He was ultimately (1890) given a brevet brigadier generalcy for service in the Indian Wars. Benteen seems to have disliked Custer at first sight; he could not bear Custer's colorful style, his show of extreme confidence, his bragging, and his ambitiousness. He may well have resented Custer's youth and his meteoric rise during the Civil War; he certainly considered Custer overrated as a military leader.[5]

A number of lesser lights were in the faction led by Benteen and Reno, but the personalities of these officers have no particular interest for one who attempts to trace the Custer story. There was also a substantial number of officers in the pro-Custer faction, and their capabilities and loyalty are significant, for most of them died at the Little Big Horn.

First of these was Custer's younger brother, Thomas Ward Custer, the captain commanding C Company. Tom was a hero worshipper where his brother was concerned, although his impetuous, fun-loving nature got him into disciplinary scrapes at times. In emulation of Custer he had joined a Michigan regiment of volunteers in 1861, when he was only sixteen. Of truly outstanding courage, he was twice awarded the Congressional Medal of Honor during the Civil War and was brevetted a lieutenant colonel. In 1864 Custer arranged for Tom to be transferred to his own command. The brothers finished the war together and later served in the Seventh Cavalry from its establishment.[6]

Another of Custer's supporters was Lt. James Calhoun, who was married to Custer's younger sister, Margaret, and whose brother was also to marry into the Custer family. Calhoun, an able officer, was in command of L Company. Capt. George Yates, who led F Company, was also a long-time Custer man. Born in New York, he had entered the Fourth Michigan Infantry during the Civil War, during one period serving on Custer's staff. There was also Capt. Myles Moylan of Company A, Calhoun's brother-in-law and a good friend of Custer's who was later awarded the Congressional Medal of Honor. Capt. Thomas Weir, who, like Yates, was from Michigan and had been with the regiment a long time, was also pro-Custer. He commanded Company D, and, although unharmed at the Little Big Horn, he did not long survive the battle, dying in December 1876.[7]

There were other elements in the Dakota column under General Terry's command in addition to the Seventh Cavalry. There was a battery of four Gatling guns, each drawn by four condemned cavalry horses (horses considered unfit for arduous maneuvers) and each capable, when functioning properly, of delivering

150 rounds of .50 caliber bullets per minute. They were operated by a platoon consisting of 1st Lt. William Low, 2d Lt. Frank Kinzie, and 32 men. There were also three companies of infantry, commanded by Captains Malcolm McArthur, Louis Sanger, and Stephen Baker, with 5 other officers and 135 men. A train of about 150 wagons managed by civilian teamsters under army contract carried supplies. Other civilians accompanying the column included Mark Kellogg, a journalist from Bismarck, North Dakota, representing not only the local paper but also the *New York Herald,* and a number of herders and foragers. Among the herders was young Harry Armstrong ("Autie") Reed, Custer's nephew. Boston Custer, Custer's youngest brother, who had been employed by the Seventh Cavalry as forage-master in 1875, was listed as a civilian guide. There was also a large detachment of scouts. About forty of these were Arikaras, including one of Custer's favorites, Bloody Knife; several Sioux; two white scouts, Fred Girard and "Lonesome Charley" Reynolds; and one black scout, Isaiah ("Teat") Dorman.[8]

The Dakota column was to rendezvous on the Yellowstone River with a column from Montana under Col. John Gibbon, consisting of five companies of infantry, a battalion of cavalry (four companies of the Second Cavalry) commanded by Maj. James Brisbin, some Crow scouts and its own supply train.[9] Three additional companies of infantry were to join the unified command at a rendezvous point in the Yellowstone country.

The entire campaign was under the commanding general of the Department of Dakota, a quiet but distinguished officer, Alfred Howe Terry. Born in Hartford, Connecticut, of an established family, he studied at Yale, practiced law for some years, and was clerk of the Supreme Court of Connecticut. His war record was exceedingly sound and, at one point—the taking of Fort Fisher, North Carolina—brilliant. He rose steadily in rank and finished his war service commanding a corps, having been brevetted a major general. Terry was twelve years older than Custer and by nature a kind and generous man, respected by both superiors and subordinates. Grant wrote of Terry in his *Memoirs* as "a man who makes friends of those under him by his consideration of their wants and their dues. As a commander, he won their confidence by his coolness in action and by his clearness of perception in taking in the situation in which he was placed at any given time." From June 1865 to August 1866, Terry commanded the Department of Virginia, a sensitive and demanding post. He was then placed in command of the Department of Dakota, having thus occupied this post (with one major interruption) for ten years at the time of the expedition against the Sioux. His duties during this period had been largely in the areas of administration and planning. Terry was not a cavalryman, and he had never led a field command against hostile Indians.[10]

It seems evident in retrospect that Terry was, from the very beginning of the expedition, in something of a quandary as to his handling of Custer. It was quite clear from Sherman's dispatch of 8 May authorizing Custer to go with his regiment on the expedition that Terry was to exercise overall command, including supervision of Custer's activities. The concluding sentence of the message read

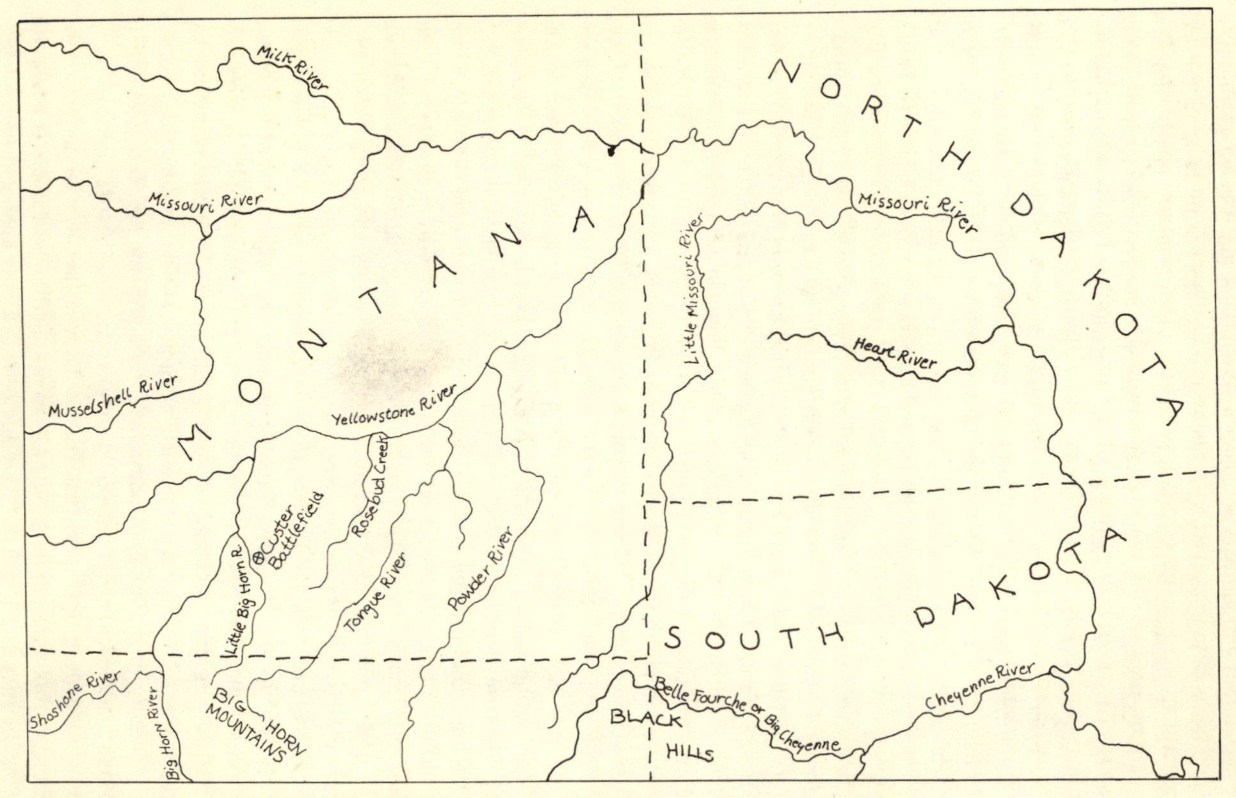

Yellowstone and Missouri River Areas, 1876. From Edgar I. Stewart, *Custer's Luck*. By *permission of the Oklahoma University Press. Copyright 1955 by the University of Oklahoma Press, Publishing Division of the University.*

"Advise Custer" —which, in this context, surely meant "order him" — "to be prudent, not to take along any newspaper men, who always make mischief, and to abstain from personalities in the future."[11] And yet Mark Kellogg was going along with the command, undoubtedly at Custer's invitation. Terry was not a publicity-seeker, and he must have agreed with Sherman's sentiments, yet he gave at least tacit approval to the newspaperman's presence. (This was not, apart from the specific circumstances, an unusual procedure: a number of newspapermen accompanied Crook on his campaign.) It seems clear that Terry's duty to follow his superior's wishes was, in this instance, overridden by his sympathy for Custer, whom he no doubt considered to have been right in aims, although very rash in means, in the matter of the Belknap impeachment. This conflict in Terry between orders to keep a tight rein on Custer and an inclination to give him his head was soon to have far-reaching effects.

The command marched almost due west from Fort Lincoln, reaching the Little Missouri River about eighty miles southwest of the point where it empties into the Missouri. Camp was made on the east bank on 29 May. As early as a week before, Custer, who always scouted ahead to find the best path for the command, had come across a still-burning Sioux campfire, and on the same day various members of the command had seen a small band of Sioux observing them from a bluff several miles away. There was little reason to doubt that the expedition was being observed by the Indians throughout much of its approach to the area in which battle was to be offered, although such observation was not part of an organized plan.

Terry had hoped that the hostiles might be found encamped in the valley of the Little Missouri (as they had been at one point during the winter), and on 30 May he sent Custer with a battalion composed of Companies C, D, F, and M and a dozen scouts on an exploration.[12] Custer went up the river valley for some twenty miles without finding any signs of recent occupancy. This reconnaissance marked the first time on the expedition that Custer had been allowed to lead troops without immediate supervision, but in view of the small number of men, it seems clear that he was not intended to bring on an engagement, but merely to gather information for Terry. After Custer's return Terry sent a dispatch to Sheridan telling him of the command's activities to that point.

On the evening of 7 June, the expedition reached the Powder River and made camp some twenty miles south of its confluence with the Yellowstone. On 8 June, scouts who had been sent north to make contact with Colonel Gibbon reported having seen a little band of Sioux who fled upon being discovered. The command rested in camp for several days, but Terry rode on to meet Gibbon and the *Far West*, a riverboat which had been engaged to bring supplies and otherwise assist the expedition from this point onward.

The dominant feature of the rugged, only partially explored country the expedition was now entering was the Yellowstone River, the longest tributary of the Missouri, rising in what is now Yellowstone National Park and running for about eleven hundred miles—first north, then east, and then north again to join the Missouri just across the western border of present-day North Dakota. In the area with which Terry's command was concerned, the Yellowstone flows eastward, receiving no significant tributaries from the north but a number of rivers and large creeks from the south, all of which were of potential strategic importance to the campaign. From east to west, these streams are the Powder River, Tongue River, Rosebud Creek (or River), Tulloch's Creek, Little Big Horn River (called "Greasy Grass" by the Indians), and the Big Horn River. Tulloch's Creek and the Little Big Horn do not, in fact, empty directly into the Yellowstone, but rather are tributaries of the Big Horn, the mount of Tulloch's Creek being a few miles upstream and that of the Little Big Horn about thirty miles upstream. The basins of these tributary streams were separated from one another by rugged hills. The valleys were fertile grazing land for buffalo and antelope and therefore good hunting ground. Between the upper reaches of the Powder and Big Horn rivers lay the Big Horn Mountains. These mountains curve to the northwest, so that a portion of the range lies west of the Big Horn River, marking the western boundary of the "unceded territory."

The Little Big Horn is a markedly winding stream, about sixty miles from source to mouth as the crow flies, but at least twice that in its frequently shifting actual course. In late summer the flow of water is reduced to a trickle, and the river can be waded across at almost any point. In the late spring, however, there are sometimes floods, and in any event the current is swift and the river five or six feet deep, fordable only at certain points. On 25 June, when, as matters turned out, Custer's command was to reach the Little Big Horn, the water seems to have averaged several feet deep with a moderate current. The banks, though of mud, were steep, and thus it was only at certain fords that a mounted column could cross the river in proper order.

The Indian village encountered by Custer lay along the west bank. It was situated upon a ledge a few feet above the river and several hundred yards wide, from which the ground sloped upward to the west, forming a plateau. The east bank was much rougher country, with a series of irregular high ridges coming fairly close to the water. The Indian encampment was extensive, consisting of several tribes whose tepees were placed in contiguous circles. The whole village was strung out along the river for a distance of more than two miles. The Sioux tribes from south to north were the Huncpapas (with their leaders, Sitting Bull, Gall, Crow King, and Black Moon); the Blackfeet; the Minneconjous (led by Hump and Lame Deer); the Sans Arcs (under Spotted Eagle); and the Ogallalas (with Crazy Horse). The northernmost circle was that of the Cheyenne, under the war chief Two Moon.

At the time there were three natural fords in this stretch of the Little Big Horn. One of these was several miles upstream from the southern end of the village, just south of where a small creek (then called Sundance Creek, and now Reno Creek) entered the river. A second was at Medicine Trail Coulee, a ravine coming down to the water's edge near the Sans Arcs and Minneconjou circles (now called the Minneconjou Ford), and the third was just north of the Cheyenne encampment.

There has been much dispute as to the number of hostile Indians Terry expected to encounter. While there is no doubt that Terry and Custer underestimated, the evidence suggests that, even before the meeting with Gibbon, they reckoned the number to be considerable. Four months earlier, Terry had written to Sheridan:

> I earnestly request that three companies of the 7th Cavalry now serving in the Department of the Gulf may be ordered to rejoin their regiment in this department. The orders which have been given recently render indispensably necessary a larger mounted force than the nine mounted companies now in this department. These nine companies comprise but six hundred and twenty men all told, and of these not over five hundred and fifty could be put in the field for active operations. This number is not sufficient for the end in view. For if the Indians who pass the winter in the Yellowstone and Powder rivers country should be found gathered in contiguous camps (and they usually are so gathered) they could not be attacked by that number without great risk of defeat.

Furthermore, just before the Dakota column started its march, Terry had sent further word to Sheridan: "It is represented that they [the hostiles] have fifteen hundred lodges, are confident, and intend making a stand."[13] The first of these messages, given the superiority of an organized cavalry formation over an equal number of Indians fighting in small autonomous groups, indicated that Terry was thinking of at least a thousand hostiles, and the second message suggests that he was at least considering the possibility of encountering several times that number. Custer, on the first day of the march up the Rosebud River, is reported by Lt. Edward S. Godfrey as having said that they would find at least one thousand, but probably not more than fifteen hundred, Indians.

In conference with Colonel Gibbon on the evening of 8 June, Terry learned in detail of all the evidence Gibbon had received of the presence of large numbers of hostile Indians south of the Yellowstone and west of the Powder. In particular he learned the results of two scouting missions made across the Yellowstone by Lt. James H. Bradley. On the first of these, Bradley had seen a great cloud of smoke in the valley of the Tongue River, estimated by his Crow scouts to represent a village of at least three hundred lodges. On the second, Bradley had himself seen a great village strung out for more than two miles in the valley of Rosebud Creek. The village obviously contained many more than three hundred lodges. Furthermore, the village first sighted had been a good thirty-five miles south of the Yellowstone, whereas the second sighting had been but half that distance from that river. In other words, the Indians, who were aware that Gibbon's command was in the general neighborhood, were showing no fear of it.[14]

Terry decided to scout the upper portions of the Powder and Tongue rivers before moving west to the Rosebud. For this purpose he sent out Major Reno with six companies of cavalry, a Gatling gun and its crew, some Arikara scouts, an exceptionally fine half-blood scout of Colonel Gibbon's named Mitch Bouyer, and a pack train of some seventy mules. Their orders were to go some distance up the Powder, cross over to the Tongue, and descend that stream to its junction with the Yellowstone, examining the various small tributaries on the way. Custer is reported to have been chagrined at not having been chosen to make this reconnaissance, and the fact was also the subject of discussion among his officers.[15] It is impossible to be sure of Terry's motives, but since Custer was not required at the camp at this point, it may well be that Terry chose Reno because he wished to appear to move gradually in giving Custer an independent command.

Reno set out on 10 June. Gibbon's command was sent back to a point on the north bank of the Yellowstone opposite the mouth of Rosebud Creek. The balance of Terry's Dakota column marched to the bank of the Powder, remaining on the south bank of the Yellowstone. At this point, Terry sent a dispatch to Sheridan.

> No Indians east of the Powder. Reno with six companies is now well up the river on his way to the Forks, whence he will cross and come down Mizpah Creek, and thence by Pumpkin Creek to Tongue River where I hope to meet him. . . . I intend then if nothing new is developed, to send Custer with nine companies of his regiment up the Tongue and then across to and down the Rosebud while the rest of the Seventh will join Gibbon and move up the Rosebud.[16]

It is to be noted that Terry did not mention sending Custer on a mission with the full regiment and that he did not specify where his headquarters would be, whether with Custer, with Gibbon, or at some third site, such as the *Far West*. It sounds rather as if Terry were testing Sheridan's reaction. Furthermore, it seems unlikely that Custer knew at this time of Terry's intention to give him an independent command. He knew as well as Terry that it had been the chief of staff's intention that he be closely supervised.

Terry ordered the infantry of the Dakota column to remain at the Powder River camp, which became in effect an advance base. The wagons were left there while the Seventh Cavalry went forward, using a pack train to permit faster movement. The regimental band stayed behind, as did many of the newest recruits. (In all, one line officer, Henry Nowlan, one veterinary surgeon, and 152 men were detached.)[17] It seems that Terry had somehow expected to acquire additional horses in the area, and, when this expectation did not materialize, he thought it better (whether on Custer's advice has not been recorded) for those going forward to have a certain number of remounts than to send on every possible man. In view of what later occurred, it is important to realize that the total number of horses and mules at Terry's disposal was considerable. Counting the Seventh Cavalry and Brisbin's battalion of the Second, there were about 850 saddle horses. There were, in addition, 72 dray horses, 16 horses for the Gatlings, and, counting Gibbon's command, probably as many as 900 mules. Terry sent forward to the mouth of the Tongue River six companies of cavalry under Custer, three Gatling guns under Low, the Arikara scouts, and the pack train.

On the evening of 19 June, word reached Terry that Major Reno had returned, having gone as far as the Rosebud valley instead of following orders. He was even then marching toward the Tongue River. Terry was angered at Reno's disobedience; he ordered him to stay where he was and sent Custer and the rest of the command on to the mouth of the Rosebud.[18] Terry himself went to the same point by steamer. Reno had undoubtedly been led by Mitch Bouyer to the place in the Rosebud valley where Lieutenant Bradley had earlier seen the large Indian village. He had, Terry learned on 20 June, followed the trail leading southward up the valley for a day and a half, but he had not been able to determine whether it turned out of the Rosebud valley, and, if it did, in which direction. Since, however, the general movement of the Dakota column had been from east to west, and since General Crook's forces were operating to the south, the odds favored a turn toward the west.

Except for the last point, which was really a surmise, Terry's understanding of the strategic problem confronting his command was not appreciably changed by Reno's report. Terry, however, decided on prompt action. On 21 June he sent a message to Sheridan.

> Traces of a large and recent camp have been discovered twenty or thirty miles up the Rosebud. Gibbon's column will move this morning . . . for the mouth of the Big Horn . . . thence it will proceed to the mouth of the Little [Big] Horn and so on. . . .
>
> Custer will go up the Rosebud tomorrow with his whole regiment and thence to the headwaters and thence down the Little [Big] Horn. . . . I only hope that one of the two columns will find the Indians. I go personally with Gibbon.[19]

This is the first mention of Custer's going with the whole Seventh Cavalry as an independent (or at least somewhat autonomous) command.

During the afternoon of the twenty-first, Terry held a council of war on board the *Far West* with Custer, Gibbon, Brisbin, and several aides. Terry's general idea was for Custer to proceed up the Rosebud until he could determine in which direction the great trail led. On the way, he was to scout both to his right and to his left. He was to explore the headwaters of Tulloch's Creek on the right, but he was to put special emphasis upon "feeling to the left," with the idea of preventing the escape in that direction of part or all of the Indians. On the basis of past experience, and despite comments of the scouts to the contrary, it seemed likely to the principal officers that the Indians would flee if they became certain of the intentions of Terry's command. If, as Terry expected, Custer were to find that the trail turned west, over the divide between the Rosebud and the Little Big Horn, he was to proceed south for some twenty miles, continuing his explorations to the left, before turning west, crossing the divide, and moving north up the Little Big Horn valley toward Gibbon. That officer, meanwhile, was to move to the Big Horn and then to the mouth of the northernmost tributary, Tulloch's Creek, exploring its reaches and going on to the mouth of the Little Big Horn. Gibbon's column would be the slower moving, since the core of the command was a battalion of infantry. It was to reach the mouth of the Little Big Horn on 26 June.[20] Major Brisbin traced out on a map the intended route of the two columns.

Terry seems to have had a very good intuitive idea of where the main body of Indians would be found. He clearly expected them to be in the Little Big Horn valley. He did not know this certainly, however, and if it were true, there would still be the question of how far up the river the main camp lay. Therefore he could not give completely definite orders. His main concern at this point seems to have been to make every effort to prevent the escape of as many Indians as possible. There is reason to suppose, however, as Terry later claimed in a dispatch to Sheridan, that he intended that his two columns be in supporting distance of one another by 26 June.[21] It seems clear that Terry's plan underestimated the mobility of the Indians, even in a village community. On the other hand, Custer, who had the broad experience in Indian fighting that Terry lacked, is not recorded by any of the participants as having emphasized uncertainties, pointed out defects in the plan, or made positive suggestions.

Edgar Stewart has remarked that "none of the three leaders seem to have even considered the possibility of defeat."[22] He may be correct, but the evidence cannot be considered conclusive. It is difficult to suppose that Terry would not have even considered the possibility that Custer's column might be defeated if forced to act alone; he had made the very clear statement to Sheridan in February that "550 men . . . were not sufficient for the end in view. . . . The Indians could not be attacked by that number without great risk of defeat."[23] Later indications suggested that the number of hostile Indians had increased rather than diminished, and the battle strength of the Seventh Cavalry was only 597 officers and men (plus 35 Indian scouts). There is, in fact, other evidence to suggest that Terry wished Custer to have every chance of success and that he was not entirely sanguine as to the chances of the Seventh Cavalry winning a victory alone. All the survivors of the Little Big Horn who had attended the conference agreed that two possibilities of strengthening Custer's column were discussed. One suggestion was that Custer might take along the Gatling guns. Another was that all the cavalry should be combined—that is, that Custer should take along Major Brisbin's battalion.[24] The merits and limitations of these suggestions will be discussed in connection with Custer's explanations to his officers for declining them, but the fact that they were made at all supports the belief that Terry was not completely confident of success if the Seventh Cavalry were to fight unsupported.

In addition to the suggestions about the Gatling guns and Brisbin's battalion, Terry indicated that he wanted Custer to take some of Brisbin's scouts, since the Arikaras were not familiar with the country. This idea Custer accepted. There were six Crows, Mitch Bouyer, and George Herendeen. Herendeen was sent along by Terry specifically to bring word of the results of the exploration of Tulloch's Creek.[25]

An interesting psychological aspect of the conference is the effect it has been generally agreed to have had upon Custer's mood. As Frederick Van de Water expressed it, "Custer had boarded the boat, elated and excited. He went ashore irritable and contagiously apprehensive."[26] Other students of Custer and the Little Big Horn fight have phrased the idea less dramatically, but no one has denied that some such change occurred. It has, indeed, been noted that going into battle against the hostile Sioux and Cheyenne was correctly perceived by most officers and men to be a very serious matter, and that a grave mood was pervasive, but this seems to be missing the point. Custer was not thought to be experiencing a lowering of spirits before the conference, and it was not at all characteristic of him to have shown indications of this afterward.

On the morning following the conference, Terry sent a message to Custer for his guidance.

Camp at Mouth of Rosebud River,
Montana Territory,
June 22d, 1876

Lieutenant-Colonel Custer,
7th Cavalry.

Colonel:

The Brigadier-General Commanding directs that, as soon as your regiment can be made ready for the march, you will proceed up the Rosebud in pursuit of the Indians whose trail was discovered by Major Reno a few days since. It is, of course, impossible to give you any definite instructions in regard to this movement, and were it not impossible to do so the Department Commander places too much confidence in your zeal, energy, and ability to wish to impose upon you precise orders which might hamper your action when nearly in contact with the enemy. He will, however, indicate to you his own views of what your action should be, and he desires that you should conform to them unless you shall see sufficient reasons for departing from them. He thinks that you should proceed up the Rosebud until you ascertain definitely the direction in which the trail above spoken of leads. Should it be found (as it appears almost certain that it will be found) to turn towards the Little Horn, he thinks that you should still proceed southward, perhaps as far as the headwaters of the Tongue, and then turn towards the Little Horn, feeling constantly, however, to your left, so as to preclude the possibility of the escape of the Indians to the south or southeast by passing around your left flank. The column of Colonel Gibbon is now in motion for the mouth of the Big Horn. As soon as it reaches that point it will cross the Yellowstone and move up at least as far as the forks of the Big and Little Horns. Of course its future movements must be controlled by circumstances as they arise, but it is hoped that the Indians, if upon the Little Horn, may be so nearly inclosed by the two columns that their escape will be impossible.

The Department Commander desires that on your way up the Rosebud you should thoroughly examine the upper part of Tulloch's Creek, and that you should endeavor to send a scout through to Colonel Gibbon's column, with information of the result of your examination. The lower part of this creek will be examined by a detachment from Colonel Gibbon's command. The supply steamer will be pushed up the Big Horn as far as the forks if the river is found to be navigable for that distance, and the Department Commander, who will accompany the column of Colonel Gibbon, desires you to report to him there not later than the expiration of the time for which your troops are rationed, unless in the meantime you receive further orders.

Very respectfully, your obedient servant,
E. W. Smith
Captain 18th Infantry
Acting Assistant Adjutant General[27]

This communication has aroused as much speculation and debate as any in American military history, and no study of the psychological forces playing upon Custer at this point, or stirred up within him, can avoid giving it extensive consideration. Both Terry's supporters and Custer's detractors (not precisely a coextensive group) have contended that it was a set of orders and that Custer disobeyed them. Custer's partisans, on the other hand, have insisted that it was only a loosely worded set of instructions and suggestions, and that consequently it is inappropriate to say that Custer defied orders. Colonel Graham, who, although he wanted to protect the army's role in general, was essentially nonpartisan in the Terry-Custer controversy, observed: "Readers should remember that to every controversial question there are two sides, and that between wilful disobedience of orders and justifiable disregard of instructions there yawns a gulf both wide and deep. . . . That Custer did disregard Terry's instructions seems reasonably clear: whether he was justified in doing so is a question that will bear examination." More recent scholars, notably Stewart and Gray, have argued persuasively that there was no major "wilful disobedience of orders," and I find their evidence convincing.[28] On the other hand, the question of unjustifiable "disregard of instructions" seems to remain open.

It is certainly fair to say that, if these were orders, they were phrased with a courtesy, a gentleness, and at one point ("unless you shall see sufficient reasons for departing from them") a tentativeness unusual in a military communication. Perhaps its tentativeness is its least remarkable feature. After all, it was not positively known whether the Indians were concentrated in a single location, or in what numbers, precisely where their encampment was, or what was the nature of the terrain. (As it turned out, the conditions proved to be just about as Terry had supposed.) Yet the unknowables of the situation could have been given due recognition in a much crisper and more directive statement. ("If this is found, do this; if that, do that; if neither, you are authorized to use your own judgment up to such-and-such a point.")

Custer himself referred to the communication as an order, and yet it has some of the characteristics of a letter of instructions. Even as such, however, the communication is unusual. It must be a rare military letter of instructions in which the commanding officer takes time out to pay direct compliments, as in "the Department Commander places too much confidence in your zeal, energy, and ability to wish to impose upon you precise orders." One is left with the conclusion that this letter is another example of Terry's doing everything possible to let Custer know that he had his commander's support. Custer certainly perceived the compliment, for, in his last letter to his wife, written immediately after receiving Terry's communication, he said: "I send you an extract from Gen'l. Terry's official order, knowing how keenly you appreciate words of commendation and confidence in your dear Bo."[29]

To complicate matters further, there has long been a controversy as to whether or not Custer received supplementary verbal orders from Terry modifying the orders, instructions, and suggestions contained in the letter and the understanding reached at the conference on the *Far West*. There is nothing inherently improbable in such an idea; however, it was not mentioned by anyone until long after the fight. In later years, as the struggle to find someone on whom to place the major blame for the debacle grew more intense, Custer partisans, notably including Lt. Gen. Nelson A. Miles when he was chief of staff, claimed that Mary Adams, the Custers' cook, had made a notarized statement in which she said that she had been present in Custer's tent when Terry walked back with him after the conference and had overheard a conversation between them.

Territory of Dakota:
ss:
County of Burleigh:

Personally came before me Mary Adams, who being first duly sworn, deposes and says: that she resides in the City of Bismarck, D.T., and has resided in said City for three months just past. That she came to Dakota Territory with General George A. Custer in the Spring of 1873. That she was in the employ of General George A. Custer continuously from 1873 up to the time of his death in June 1876. That while in his employ she accompanied him on his military expeditions in the capacity of cook. That she left Fort A. Lincoln in the Spring of 1876 with Gen'l. Terry's expedition in the employ of the said General Custer, and was present in the said General Custer's tent on the Rosebud River in Montana Territory when General Terry came into said tent, and the said Terry said to General Custer: "Custer, I don't know what to say for the last." Custer replied, "Say whatever you want to say." Terry then said, "Use your own judgement and do what you think best if you strike the trail. And whatever you do, Custer, hold on to your wounded" and further saith not.

her
x
Mary Adams
mark

Subscribed and sworn to
before me this 16th day of
January, 1878.
[notarial seal][30]

It is generally agreed that an unidentified officer did eventually take Mary Adams to a notary public in Bismarck to make this statement. Moreover, although Graham produced evidence indicating that Mary was back at Fort Abraham Lincoln at the time of the Battle of the Little Big Horn, there now is contradictory evidence that she went along on the expedition, remaining on the *Far West* when the regiment went toward its final action. Lawrence Frost has seen letters from Boston Custer and from Armstrong Reed, written on the expedition and referring in passing to the presence of the cook. However, it remains highly improbable that the notarized statement is an accurate reflection of what occurred. In the first place, it is entirely out of keeping with Terry's attitude and manner toward Custer that he would have made such a cautioning, if not insulting, remark as "whatever you do,

Custer, hold on to your wounded.'' In the second place, it is highly unlikely that an uneducated person would have perceived, let alone retained for one-and-one-half years, the polished phrasing of the conversation, including, for example, an expression such as ''I don't know what to say for the last.'' Finally, had such a document been an accurate reflection of events, it would surely not have been hidden away by Custer partisans throughout the remainder of Terry's life. The whole thing has the appearance of a fabrication constructed after the fact to meet a highly controversial situation.

It should be noted that General Miles, in his defense of Custer (a close personal friend), made more of the Mary Adams affidavit than he did of inferences to be drawn from Terry's communication or the circumstances on the Little Big Horn as Custer found them. If this evidence lacks credibility, as seems to be the case, Mile's commentary comes close to being a tacit and unwilling admission on the part of this strong Custer partisan that Custer did, in fact, disregard the intentions of Terry's letter without sufficient reasons.

After the *Far West* conference Custer called a meeting of his officers. He told them of the march up the Rosebud, which by now everyone was expecting. He ordered that fifteen days' rations of bread and twelve of bacon be taken in the pack train; he also directed that a supply of salt be taken along, indicating that the regiment would follow the Indians, no matter how far or in what direction the trail led them, and that they might have to subsist on horse meat. An extra supply of forage also was to be taken. At this, two of the officers protested, evidently showing surprise at preparations for so extended a march and expressing fear that the extra weight might cause some of the pack mules to break down.

The regiment moved out at noon on Thursday, 22 June. Terry, Custer, Gibbon, and Brisbin watched the men pass in review. Custer shook hands with the other officers and started to ride off to take his place at the head of the column. As he did so, Gibbon called after him, ''Now Custer, don't be greedy! Wait for us!'' ''No, I will not!'' replied Custer ambiguously and rode away.[31]

The regiment halted at 4:00 P.M., Chicago time, having traveled about fourteen miles.[32] Toward sunset, officers' call was sounded on the bugle. Lieutenant Godfrey's eyewitness account recreates the circumstances of the expedition.

It was not a cheerful assemblage; everybody seemed to be in a serious mood, and the little conversation carried on, before all had arrived, was in undertones. When all had assembled, the General said that until further orders, trumpet calls would not be sounded except in an emergency; the marches would begin at five a.m. sharp; the troop commanders were all experienced officers, and knew well enough what to do, and when to do what was necessary for their troops; there were two things that would be regulated from his headquarters, i.e., when to move out of and when to go into camp. All other details, such as reveille, stables, watering, halting, grazing, etc., on the march would be left to the judgement and discretion of the troop commanders; they were to keep within supporting distance of each other, not to get ahead of the scouts, or very far to the rear of the column. He took particular pains to impress upon the officers his reliance upon their judgement, discretion, and loyalty. He thought, judging from the number of lodgefires reported by Reno, that we might meet at least

1,000 warriors; there might be enough men from the agencies, visiting their hostile friends, to make a total of 1,500. He had consulted the reports of the Commissioner of Indian Affairs and the officials while in Washington as to the probable number of "Hostiles" (those who had persistently refused to live or enroll themselves at the Indian agencies), and he was confident, if any reliance was to be placed upon these reports, that there would not be an opposing force of more than 1,500. General Terry had offered him the additional force of the battalion of the 2nd Cavalry, but he had declined it because he felt sure that the 7th Cavalry could whip any force that would be able to combine against him, that if the regiment could not, no other regiment in the service could; if they could whip the regiment, they would be able to defeat a much larger force, or, in other words, the reinforcements of this battalion could not save us from defeat. With the regiment acting alone, there would be harmony, but another organization would be sure to cause jealousy or friction. He had declined the offer of the Gatling guns for the reason that they might hamper our movements or march at a critical moment, because of the inferior horses and of the difficult nature of the country through which we would march. The marches would be from twenty-five to thirty miles a day. Troop officers were cautioned to husband their rations and the strength of their mules and horses, as we might be out for a great deal longer time than that for which we were rationed, as he intended to follow the trail until we could get the Indians, even if it took us to the Indian agencies on the Missouri River or in Nebraska. All officers were requested to make to him any suggestion they thought fit.

This "talk" of his, as we called it, was considered at the time as something extraordinary for General Custer, for it was not his habit to unbosom himself to his officers. In it he showed concessions and a reliance on others; there was an indefinable something that was not Custer. His manner and tone, usually brusque and aggressive, or somewhat curt, was on this occasion conciliating and subdued. There was something akin to an appeal, as if depressed, that made a deep impression on all present. We compared watches to get the official time, and separated to attend to our various duties. Lieutenants McIntosh, Wallace (killed at the Battle of Wounded Knee, December 29, 1890), and myself walked to our bivouac, for some distance in silence, when Wallace remarked: "Godfrey, I believe General Custer is going to be killed." "Why, Wallace," I replied, "What makes you think so?" "Because," said he, "I have never heard Custer talk in that way before."[33]

Godfrey's account of Custer's unaccustomed mood and manner can stand for the present without comment; otherwise, he reports nothing exceptional. Custer's orders were routine under the circumstances and only noteworthy for the way in which they were coupled with his comment about placing reliance upon the judgment, discretion, and loyalty of his officers, a very clear echo of Terry's letter of instructions.

Custer's explanations of his reasons for declining Brisbin's battalion and the Gatling guns, however, require some discussion. They were not untrue, but they did not convey the whole truth. Custer did have great pride in the Seventh Cavalry, and the Gatling guns could not have kept pace with a regiment of horse on forced marches. Nonetheless, the attempts often made to defend Custer's decisions on a purely rational basis are somewhat strained. It has frequently been emphasized that the Gatling guns were pulled by "condemned cavalry horses"; that Reno had reported that the gun sent along with him could not keep up with the pace of his reconnaissance; that the guns were insufficiently mobile to be useful in offensive maneuvers; and that they overheated when fired continuously, causing the bullets to become jammed in the barrels. But there are valid responses to each of these objections. First, Terry had at his disposal something like 1,800 horses and mules, and it would therefore have been a relatively easy matter to select 16 sound draft animals if Custer had wanted the Gatlings. Second, while Reno's gun could not keep up with his cavalry companies, it had pretty well kept up with his pack train (which was where it belonged), and it had managed to finish the forced march. Third, Gatling guns were not intended primarily for offense, but they would have been valuable defensively if the pack train were attacked—a contingency for which Custer later was to provide in a very costly manner. They could be similarly valuable to an entire regiment if it were forced on the defensive, a contingency which, while not expected, could not logically be eliminated. These guns, each capable of firing 150 rounds per minute,[34] would have strongly increased the firepower of the regiment, particularly if one considers the usual custom of detaching every fourth trooper as a horse-holder. Finally, while it was true that the Gatling guns tended to overheat with extended use, so did the troopers' carbines. Beyond these considerations, there was the further point that most of the Indians were unused to facing such weapons; the guns could have had a shock effect well beyond their actual destructive potential.

The reasons for Custer's refusal to take all or any of Brisbin's cavalry are similarly unclear. Some authorities have insisted that Custer wanted the expected fight to be exclusively a Seventh Cavalry affair. However, commanders rarely consider it a slight to have their forces enlarged. A considerable part of the explanation for Custer's refusal (although he did not acknowledge it) probably was his belief that if Brisbin's troops had gone along with the Seventh Cavalry Terry would have gone also, thus depriving Custer of his autonomy.[35] Since Terry was not a cavalryman and was not inured to the hardships of days in the saddle on a rapid march, his accompanying Custer was not a certainty. Furthermore, in view of Terry's strong inclination to give Custer an independent command, it is possible that Custer might have taken at least a company of Brisbin's cavalry without Terry's feeling in duty bound to go along. (And, if Custer were to divide his forces into battalions, as he of course did, the addition of even a single company would have increased the offensive power of any one battalion by about one-third.) Custer probably could not have accepted both the Gatlings and Brisbin's cavalry without Terry's feeling that his presence was mandatory, yet this circumstance does not really explain his refusal to take advantage of either offer.

FOUR

Approach and Battle

CUSTER'S command moved out early on the morning of Friday, 23 June. Soon afterward it passed the large campsite that Major Reno had noted on his scout. Other campsites were later noted, and eventually the trail Custer followed became impressive in its size, being heavily worn and some 300 yards wide. The scouts (probably overestimating) said that this single trail had been made by about 1,500 lodges, which would indicate a fighting force of at least 3,000 warriors.[1] Custer somehow was not impressed by the steady widening of the trail and persisted in the belief that the village sites were the successive camping places of a single group of Indians, rather than the separate camps of groups moving toward a rendezvous. The regiment moved rapidly this second day, having covered something over thirty miles when it went into camp. Some of the officers reported having seen smoke signals during the march, although there was no general agreement on this point. In retrospect, it seems possible that the command was under occasional observation by the hostiles during its march up the Rosebud.[2]

Soon after the regiment began its march on the morning of the twenty-fourth, there was evidence to this effect. The Crow scouts reported fresh tracks of Sioux ponies nearby. A bit later one of the Crows reported having seen a Sioux scout. Still later, at a large campsite, the Crows noticed pictograms, which they said indicated that the Sioux knew that the command was approaching. No attempt was made to scout the upper reaches of Tulloch's Creek as Terry had ordered.[3] This neglect has been excused by some students of the campaign on the ground that the area in question was not suitable for the location of a sizable village. On the other hand, Terry had not maintained that it would be.

In the afternoon, the regiment encountered another Indian trail coming up from the south and joining the one being followed. Moreover, the trail was freshening; by studying various indications, including the pony droppings, the scouts could report that the regiment was catching up; the Indians could not be very far ahead. At this time Scout Herendeen asked Custer for permission to begin his ride back to Terry to report the situation as ordered. The permission was not granted.[4]

The command went into camp shortly before 8:00 P.M. on Saturday, having covered another thirty miles. By now, Custer had moved approximately seventy-five miles in fifty-six hours, and he was somewhat ahead of the schedule as marked out on the map at the conference on the *Far West*. Terry presumably would have expected him to rest the command overnight and then to move a good bit farther south on the following day, while scouting ahead, to the left, and to the right. Custer, however, had other ideas. Even before the command halted, he had sent ahead some of the Crows to determine the direction of the Indian trail. About 9:00 P.M. they returned with the information that the trail turned to the right (west) and crossed the divide separating the valley of the Rosebud from that of the Little Big Horn. Custer at once decided on a night march. He had been told of an excellent lookout spot, the rounded top of a high hill at the crest of the divide called the Crow's Nest, from which one could see far up and down the Little Big Horn valley, and he now ordered Lieutenant Varnum, Mitch Bouyer, Charlie Reynolds, several Crows, and several Arikaras to see if they could locate the Indian village either by campfires during the night or by smoke at dawn.[5]

Custer ordered a night march to start at 11:00 P.M., and he announced his intention of getting as close as possible to the divide before daybreak and then hiding there all day on the twenty-fifth.[6] During this time the scouts would determine the nature of the intervening terrain, and the regiment would attack at dawn on 26 June. The decision not to follow the Rosebud farther south was the third instance in which Custer disregarded—or, depending upon one's point of view, disobeyed—Terry's instructions.

There was no assurance that there would be a satisfactory place of concealment for the regiment after this further advance. Moreover, there was no clear-cut gain to be made by it. The horses would have been no more fatigued, and probably less, if the few miles gained toward the objective had been added on to the final advance after twenty-four hours' rest. Certainly the pass through which the regiment intended to cross the intervening hills could have been adequately guarded from the position of its evening halt, provided that an observation party had been sent forward. Yet the plan was not really a bad one, and had Terry been present, he might perhaps have agreed to it. Discussing Custer's conscious motivations at this time, Stewart has said persuasively:

> A fair guess would be that Custer was determined that the credit for winning a great victory over the hostile tribes should go to him and his regiment alone. To delay too long meant that the glory might have to be shared with Terry and Gibbon. To continue south towards the headwaters of the Tongue River—as Terry had suggested—meant that he might encounter General Crook, in which case he would be outranked and would become merely a subordinate commander in a larger enterprise, so that the credit for crushing the Sioux would go to others.[7]

The regiment moved up the valley of a small tributary of the Rosebud, probably Davis Creek. The advance was difficult and slow. Moreover, while night marchers did not have to be concerned about stirring up dust, this advantage was at least balanced by the problem of men straying from the trail and troopers having to bang on their saddles with tin cups or other implements to guide those behind them. Occasionally also a horse would lose its footing and fall with a crash. As Frederick Van de Water put it, "Any Indian in a range of several miles and not stone deaf must have heard that uproarious advance." The command had managed to advance six miles or so when it halted at about 2:00 A.M. While waiting for dawn and word from the lookout at the Crow's Nest, Custer conferred with some of the scouts who had remained with the command. Fred Girard said at that time that he expected the number of hostiles encamped somewhere across the divide would be not less than 2,500.[8]

With the coming of dawn, the Indian scouts at the Crow's Nest saw to the northwest unmistakable evidence of a huge Indian camp. Details could not be made out at the distance, some fifteen miles or more, but there was the haze from countless campfires and a sense of movement, like "worms crawling in the grass," which indicated the stirrings of a vast pony herd. Charley Reynolds said, "That's the biggest pony herd any man ever saw." "Biggest village," added Mitch Bouyer. "A heap too big." Lieutenant Varnum, his eyes tired from lack of sleep, could not see these indications, but he believed the experienced scouts, and he sent a courier to give Custer the news.[9]

Custer had the regiment on the move by about 8:45 on Sunday morning, 25 June. After advancing some four miles they halted, while Custer rode on to the Crow's Nest. He looked searchingly in the direction pointed out by the scouts, but professed to see no indication of the Indian village. It is possible that he did not, for conditions had changed. The scouts had made their observations in the early morning, when the earth was not warmed by the sun. Now, at 10:30 or so, there was a shimmering haze over the valley. Bouyer assured him that the village was the largest ever seen on the plains. Custer returned to the command and was then given other reports. Several of the scouts said that they had seen two small war parties observing the regiment from a distance and then riding off in the general direction of the village reported from the Crow's Nest. Herendeen had also seen a warrior at a range of several hundred yards observing the command. Moreover, Sgt. William Curtis and two men of F Company, who had ridden back along the trail to recover some provisions dropped during the night march, had found an Indian examining them, who rode off at the approach of the troopers.[10]

It was clear, then, that the hostiles would soon be informed of the location of the regiment. There was a fair amount of evidence that at least some bands of the Indians had been aware that forces were moving against them for some time, very possibly for a number of days. If Bouyer and the other scouts at the Crow's Nest were correct, Custer's command was now closer to a large encampment of the hostiles than at any previous time. Yet there was no clear indication to the Indians that their village or villages had been discovered by the whites, and, moreover, the command was at this time some fifteen or more miles away by riding trail from the encampment the scouts had claimed existed. At this point Custer made what seems a paradoxical decision. While declaring to his officers that he did not believe that there was a village down the Little Big Horn valley, he made preparations for an attack upon it.[11] He first ordered the scouts to ride ahead and to stampede the pony herd. Then he organized a guard for the pack train. McDougall's Company B was assigned for this purpose, and to it were added a noncommissioned officer and 6 men from each of the other companies. The 129 officers and men (plus 7 civilians) thus assigned were a significant fraction of the regiment, comprising more than one-fifth of its total strength and leaving only 468 officers and men (plus 47 others) for a more rapid advance.[12]

At almost exactly 12:00, Sunday, 25 June, the regiment crossed the divide and began the descent into the Little Big Horn valley; at roughly the same time Varnum and the scouts returned from the Crow's Nest. The command was moving slowly down toward the mouth of a small tributary of the Little Big Horn, Sundance (now Reno) Creek. Varnum told Custer that he had seen a band of Indians which had been encamped across the Little Big Horn near the mouth of the creek break up and begin moving downstream. After having moved less than a mile, Custer halted the regiment and divided his forces into battalions. Companies H, D, and K, commanded by Benteen, Weir, and Godfrey respectively, were placed under the command of Benteen, the senior captain. Companies A, G, and M (Moylan, McIntosh, and French) were given to Reno. Companies C (Tom Custer), E (Smith), F (Yates), I (Keogh), and L (Calhoun) were retained by Custer under his personal command. It seems likely that Custer's wing was further divided into two battalions, under Yates and Keogh respectively. Benteen was given verbal instructions to move out from the trail down Reno Creek at a "left oblique," that is, at an angle of forty-five degrees, and, according to Benteen's later report, "to pitch into" any Indians that might be found. Supplementary verbal orders, sent after Benteen by courier, were to the effect that he was to scout as far as the second line of bluffs lying before him and then return to the valley.[13]

Custer's splitting of his small command into several fragments, like others of his activities and decisions, has been both criticized and stoutly defended, with the missions of Benteen and Reno generating the most commentary. However, the assignment of such a relatively large guard to the pack train merits attention. At the time this decision was made, there was considerable evidence that a large body of hostile Indians lay somewhere ahead. At what must then have been Custer's lowest estimate, there were perhaps 1,000 warriors, and perhaps three times that number according to the estimates of the scouts. There was no evidence that any sizable body of warriors was operating close to the rear of the command. Even if a small band of hostile raiders had been overlooked and attacked the pack train, the guard was excessive. On the other hand, if a major village or several villages had somehow been missed, it was inadequate. In any case, the detachment of so many men left the rest of the command facing odds of more than two to one at best and of more than six to one if the scouts proved correct.

Benteen's scout to the left has been defended on the grounds that Custer wished to prevent the escape of the Indians sighted from the Crow's Nest up the Little Big Horn valley to the south. Yet there was no sign of any such movement; moreover, Custer and Reno were approaching the valley by a closer route than that assigned to

Benteen. Gray has suggested that Custer envisioned the strong possibility that there might be satellite villages considerably upstream from the point where Reno Creek entered the Little Big Horn, and that the mission of Benteen's battalion was to deal with or at least to observe and report back on these.[14] This idea seems somewhat more reasonable—Custer might have thought along these lines—yet it is not entirely logical either. The terrain over which Benteen would have had to march to reach the Little Big Horn valley was very rocky and uneven, a succession of ridges and valleys, and he would have to cross four little streams. Although the straight-line distance between the battalion's point of departure from the trail and the Little Big Horn valley is only about eleven miles along the angle chosen, a body of horsemen would have had to cover much more than this to reach the valley, and the mounts would have reached it nearly exhausted. Fighting would have been difficult. A large village could not have been overcome, and a war party could not have been pursued. As for observation, Benteen would have had to go considerably farther than he did in order to get an extensive view of the valley. If he had done so, regardless of what he might have seen, the time consumed would have rendered him useless to the rest of the command for several hours.

Benteen himself later said of his mission:

> But through the whole oblique to the left, the impression went through me that all of that hard detour was for naught, as the ground was too awfully rugged for sane Indians to choose to go that way to hunt a camp—or, for that matter, to hunt anything else but game.
>
> I knew that I had to come to some decision speedily, when I had given up the idea of further hunting for a valley and being thoroughly impregnated with the belief that the trail Custer was on would yield quite a sufficiency of Indians.[15]

The idea that any Indians who might be encamped upstream would have come over Benteen's route is gratuitous, but the comments give an idea of the difficulty of the terrain and the advisability of the regiment's being united.

Stewart has given what seems a good estimate of Custer's conscious motivation at this juncture.

> Although Custer did not, so far as we know, explain its purpose or the reasons behind [Benteen's mission] to anyone, this division of the command undoubtedly originated in that part of General Terry's instructions which directed Custer to keep feeling constantly to his left in order to keep the hostiles from passing around that flank and escaping to the south and west.[16]

In other words, Custer, belatedly and in a different context, was making a gesture of compliance with Terry's wishes. As events proved, it was a costly gesture.

Benteen and his three companies headed to the left at about 12:15 and were lost to sight by 12:30. The remainder of the regiment continued down the valley of Reno Creek for several miles in a single column of fours; then, when space permitted, Reno crossed over to the opposite side and both units rode on in parallel formations. When the valley widened still further, Custer ordered Reno to rejoin him on the right bank. When they had gone about eleven miles from the divide,

Custer's wing encountered a couple of tepees, the larger and more imposing of which was covered with paintings and contained the body of a dead warrior.[17] The site—a convenient reference point—has become known in the history of the Little Big Horn fight as the Lone Tepee or the Lone Warrior Tepee. It had been occupied until that very morning. Some of the scouts whom Custer earlier had sent on ahead had lingered there, and the whole command paused briefly.

From this point on the trail, Custer and Reno could see some distance into the Little Big Horn valley, although the area to the right (north) was shortly obscured by hills on the near side of the stream and by trees along both banks. In this direction, perhaps four miles downstream, a substantial cloud of dust could be seen, indicating Indian ponies in motion. Fred Girard, who had been making observations from a small hill just to the north of the Lone Warrior Tepee, rode up and called out, "There go your Indians, running like devils!" He had seen a group of approximately forty warriors on the near side of the Little Big Horn, riding to the north. It is unclear whether this small group was responsible for the dust cloud.[18] Custer and his officers naturally were keyed up and, perhaps not quite so naturally, were obsessed with the idea that the principal tactical problem was to prevent the flight of the main Indian encampment which was supposed to be in the valley on the far side of the river.

At any rate, Custer ordered the Arikaras to cross the river and move toward the dust cloud with the object of stampeding the horses of the hostiles. The scouts hesitated—they knew that the Sioux and Cheyenne were assembled in great force, and they did not want to go forward alone. Custer now gave Major Reno an order, probably through W. W. Cooke, the adjutant, to take his battalion, cross the Little Big Horn, and give battle. The precise wording of this order may never be known, for Cooke died with Custer, and Reno, when testifying later at the court of inquiry, was under great pressure to justify himself. Still, it seems likely that the verbal orders took some such form as "Charge the Indians where you find them, and you will be supported by the whole outfit." Virtually all students of the battle agree that these orders were absolute; that is, they were not discretionary, and they left Reno no alternative to sustaining an attack. A majority of the scouts went with Reno, and he thus had under his command 175 men, 140 cavalry men and officers and 35 scouts.[19] At the time of Custer's order, probably about 2:15, the pack train under McDougall was about six miles to the rear on the trail, and Benteen's battalion, having completed its scout and rejoined the trail, was about four-and-one-half miles back. These were not great distances, and yet, in terms of a fast-moving offensive, they were too great to permit effective support.

Reno moved briskly toward the river, traversing the three-mile distance in some fifteen minutes. The battalion crossed smoothly at a natural ford lying almost in the path of advance. Captain Keogh and Lieutenant Cooke rode to the ford with Reno. Girard and some of the scouts had preceded the battalion across the river, and they soon became aware that the Indians down the valley were not fleeing, as had at first been supposed, but were advancing toward the battalion. Girard reported the observation to Reno, and thinking that Custer should also be apprised, he shouted the news to Cooke.[20]

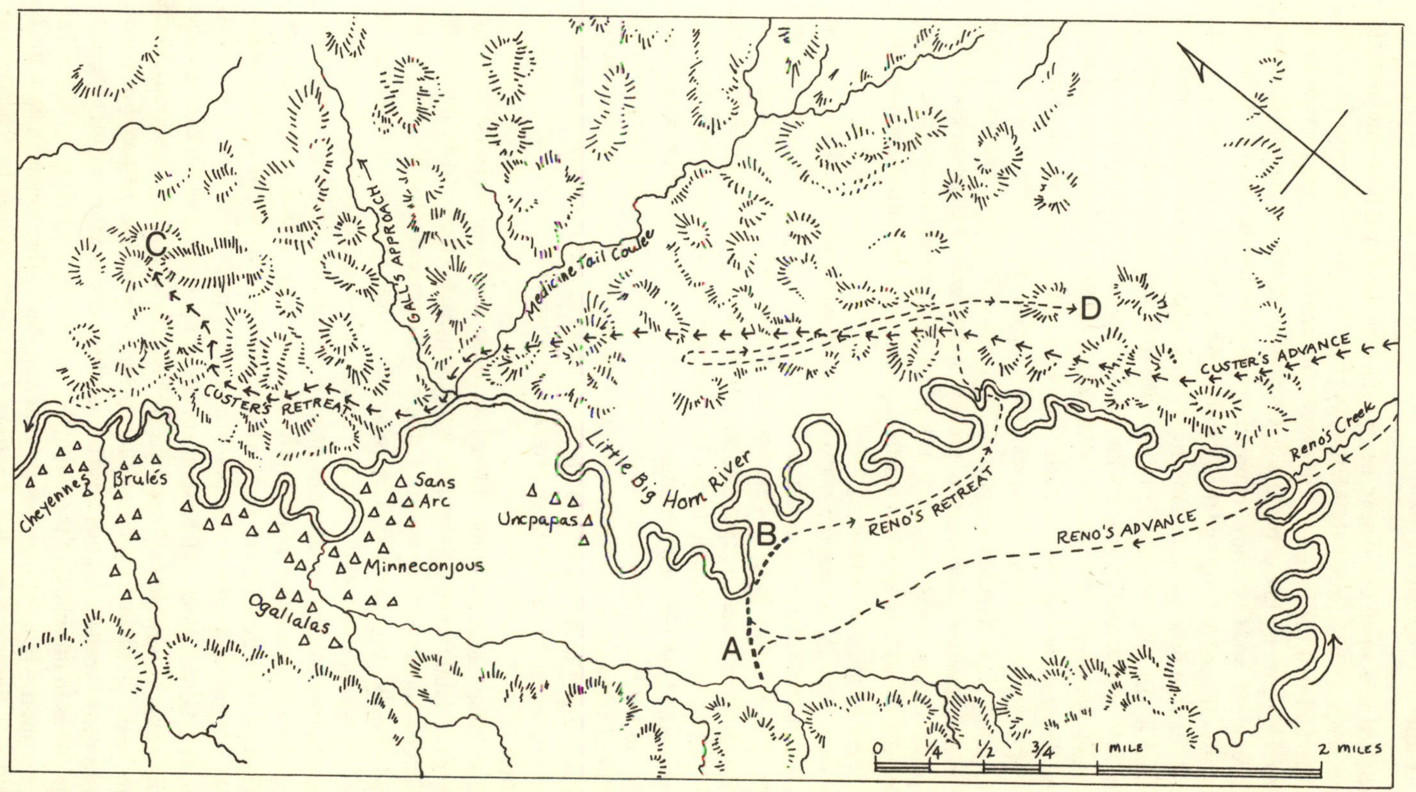

The Battle of the Little Big Horn. *A* indicates Major Reno's initial position; *B* indicates his second position. After the map based on one made by Lt. Edward S. Godfrey in Edgar I. Stewart, *Custer's Luck. By permission of the Oklahoma University Press. Copyright 1955 by the University of Oklahoma Press, Publishing Division of the University.*

Reno halted in a small wood near the crossing and reformed his command. He sent a messenger, Pvt. Archibald McIlhargy, back across the river to Custer to confirm the fact that the Indians were moving upstream, and then moved out to meet them. He formed a line of battle with Companies A and M, placing the scouts on his extreme left and Company G immediately behind him in reserve. He led the advance himself, first at a trot and then a gallop. Ahead was the large and growing dust cloud, caused now by the Indians racing their ponies in wheeling maneuvers and making it virtually impossible to estimate their number. After advancing a mile or so, Reno ordered G Company into the line, but continued moving forward without slackening pace. The Indians, who had almost certainly observed Custer's command descending into the Little Big Horn valley along Reno Creek, were not, as many of them were later to claim, taken by surprise. They were in fact moving forward against Reno's battalion in considerable force. Reno and his men, both in the event and in their later reports, greatly overestimated their number. Yet, though probably not more than one-fourth of the warrior population of the village was involved, Reno's troopers eventually faced 500 or more braves and were thus outnumbered by about four to one.[21]

For a short time the advance was maintained in good order, and the initiative remained with the battalion. Then things began to happen which altered the entire situation. The Arikaras on Reno's extreme left pulled out of the line in accordance with their assigned role, to find and stampede any unguarded portions of the hostiles' pony herd. Whether Reno had understood that this would be their function is not clear, but their departure left that end of his line unprotected, and, since the valley had widened somewhat, there now was plenty of room for the more daring Indians to ride around the line and begin circling in. Reno sent a second messenger back seeking aid from Custer and then immediately dismounted his men, sending the horses to his right rear close to the river, and formed a skirmish line.[22]

In view of the menacing horde of Indians, whose resistance was now stiffening, there were certainly some good arguments to be made for Reno's decision; yet the cost was considerable. For one thing, the move transferred the initiative to the mounted enemy. For another, it considerably reduced the battalion's fighting power. One trooper went to the rear as a holder for every four horses, and thus the number of those in the line after this maneuver could not have much exceeded a hundred. Still, it was easier to aim and to take advantage of the minimal cover the field afforded once the battalion was on the ground, and the advance continued for a couple of hundred years. At the point of maximum advance, Reno's men were within a few hundred yards of the southern end of the village, and in fact a number of its inhabitants were killed by stray carbine bullets. Among those thus killed were the wife and two children of Gall, principal war chief of the Huncpapas, whose tepees formed the southern end of the village and who formed the core of the warrior forces in this phase of the battle.[23]

After a short while, perhaps twenty minutes, Reno's line began to cave in. To the right and rear was a wooded spot of ground, partly secured by a curve of the river and affording a better defensive position than the open field. Whether the line was ordered to reform there or whether it simply drifted back to it under constant Indian pressure is a matter of question, but it did retreat and held this spot of timber for a time. Incredible as it sounds, Reno's casualties up to this point had been very slight. Thousands of rounds had been fired on both sides, and yet not more than two or three of the troopers seem to have been killed.[24] Still, the situation was harrowing in the extreme. Reno had had no previous experience in combat with Indians; his nerves were on edge; he was disappointed, astonished, and on the verge of demoralization at not having seen the slightest sign of support from Custer. The time that had elapsed since his crossing the river and beginning his advance must have seemed endless, although in fact it was probably no more than one hour.[25] Had there been a sense of trust and mutual respect between Reno and Custer, Reno might have borne these frightening experiences in a more soldierly fashion—he had, after all, faced death more than once in the Civil War—but this was not the case.

The spot into which the battalion retreated was well suited to defense. Nearly every critic of the battle believes that it could have been held by a resolute commander for a number of hours; with proper conservation of ammunition it might have been defended much longer. However, partly because of Reno's fear, partly because of a shortage of seasoned noncommissioned officers, and partly because a sprinkling of the men had not previously been under enemy fire, such control was not exercised, and ammunition was dwindling rapidly. Moreover, both individual and small groups of warriors were beginning to infiltrate the timber and fire upon the troopers and horses from various directions. The casualties remained very light; here and there a man or a horse was wounded; but Reno found the tension unbearable. He became convinced of the necessity to retreat. Near the center of the little wooded area was a clearing, and here Reno gave an order to saddle up and be prepared to ride out. It is a measure of his mounting fear and disorganization that the order was given vocally and not by bugle call. As a result, some of the men did not hear it. As those who did were preparing for the evacuation, a sizable number of warriors managed to penetrate the woods and fire a volley. A trooper and the scout Bloody Knife were hit. The latter, who was within a few yards of Reno, was struck in the head, and the major was spattered with blood and brains. Reno seems to have been so unnerved that he ordered the battalion to dismount and then immediately to remount.[26]

Reno placed himself at the head of the troopers nearest him, who were chiefly from A Company, and started out of the woods and toward the ford by which the battalion had crossed the Little Big Horn a scant hour and a quarter earlier. He gave no thought to the dead and wounded, and, because orders were not given by bugle, he also left behind Lieutenants McIntosh and DeRudio and perhaps as many as fifteen able-bodied troopers. The battalion moved out of the timber in a column of fours, but no semblance of order was maintained for long. The Indians, at first taken by surprise at the retreat, quickly adjusted to the situation. They rode alongside the column's right flank, pumping shots into the fleeing troopers and their horses and causing heavy casualties. This pressure was so strong and the leadership of the column so disorganized that there was no chance of reaching the original ford. The column veered continually to the left and reached the river over a mile short of their destination. Here the banks were steep, but the terrified men and horses plunged in, taking further casualties, but for the most part managing to get across. Lt. Benjamin Hodgson, Reno's adjutant and a favorite of the regiment, was shot in crossing and killed after he had reached the opposite bank.[27] What was left of the battalion struggled up the hill on the east side of the river. Reno was too demoralized to attempt any sort of rearguard action or even to cover the retreat of the last elements of the column by organizing fire from those first to arrive on the bluffs. It was about 4:00 P.M. when the greater part of the routed column had established itself upon the heights known since then as Reno Hill. The Sioux, had they immediately pursued Reno's command across the river, could have wiped it out, but they did not. For reasons which shortly will become apparent, even the firing from across the river slackened and became sporadic.[28]

Benteen's scout was uneventful. His battalion encountered not a single hostile Indian. The going was very rough, and it was not much longer than an hour (although some of the officers and men overestimated the time considerably) before he regained the main trail, having turned at a "right oblique." Just as he was going to do so (at about 2:20), he and some of the others saw Boston Custer riding along at a slow gallop to overtake Custer's unit. The younger Custer succeeded in doing this, and, with Armstrong Reed, who had accompanied Custer's personal command from the time the regiment was divided that morning, he was soon to perish on Custer Hill.[29] A mile or so farther down the main trail, Benteen came to a spring. He halted the battalion and allowed the thirsty horses to drink. He moved out again at about 2:50—that is to say, at almost the same time that Reno, riding down the far side of the Little Big Horn valley, came in sight of the hostiles. In fact, a few moments earlier, some of the officers had thought that they heard shots from the valley. Captain Weir, a loyal Custer supporter, became uneasy at this and urged Benteen to start immediately. Benteen was a bit slow to respond, and Weir mounted up D Company and started it moving. Benteen then set the rest of the battalion in motion down the trail.[30]

The unit passed the Lone Warrior Tepee without halting. Not long afterward it encountered a courier, Sgt. Daniel Kanipe, riding toward it at a gallop. Kanipe was carrying verbal orders for McDougall, commander of the pack train, telling him to rush the train forward. Benteen listened to the orders and then sent the messenger to the rear, telling him that he believed the pack train was a few miles back.[31] The battalion moved on for perhaps another fifteen minutes, reaching a spot about a mile from the river and about the same distance south of Reno Hill. Here it encountered Trumpeter John Martin, another messenger sent back by Custer. Martin, whose horse had been shot, was not moving as fast as Kanipe.

Martin handed Benteen a quickly scrawled message:

> Benteen—
> Come on. Big

village. Be quick
bring packs.

W. W. Cooke

P.S. Bring pacs.[32]

Benteen read the message and asked Martin, "Where's the general?" Martin replied that Custer had just encountered a force of Indians in a ravine leading down to the river as he (Martin) was riding away, and he gave it as his opinion that the Indians were "skedaddling." Benteen showed the message to Weir, but he asked for no comments and Weir gave none. Benteen did not act on this order. It is understandable that he would have been puzzled by the message. If Custer were pursuing the Indians or in a running fight with them, supplies could not be distributed. If not—well, Kanipe had already brought orders to the train to move forward as fast as possible. Yet it is remarkable that Benteen did not perceive at least some of the significance of the order, or, if he did, that he did not act on the cues presented. For one thing, the hasty writing, the incomplete sentences, the misspelling, and the unintended repetition gave every indication that Custer's immediate command was in trouble, or at the very least under extreme pressure. For another, the reiterated order, "Bring packs," coming swiftly on Kanipe's message, "Hurry up the pack train," surely meant a shift in emphasis. "Packs," one would expect Benteen to have recognized, meant something more specific, "ammunition packs."[33]

As a matter of fact, because of Benteen's detour to the left and his slow progress, the pack train was now actually in sight, not much more than a mile behind the battalion. Martin was not sent on to it, however, nor was anyone else from Benteen's command. As sounds of firing a short distance ahead were now clearly and persistently heard, the battalion quickened its pace and left the train farther behind.[34] Benteen soon came into the valley and had a clear view northward.

The first thing the battalion saw was a small group of troopers on the far side of the river, dismounted, firing, and being overwhelmed by a mass of Indians. These were men left by Reno in his dash for safety. On the near side of the Little Big Horn were some Arikara scouts with captured Sioux ponies. They indicated that most of Reno's soldiers were on a hill to the right. Toward this Benteen led his battalion, and soon approached Reno and the remnants of his command. Reno went forward to meet him, looking haggard and completely distraught. He had lost his hat, and his head was tied around with a bandana. He cried out, "For God's sake, Benteen, halt your command and help me. I've lost half my men." In reply to Benteen's question as to Custer's whereabouts, Reno said that the general had headed north (downstream) with five companies and had not been heard from.[35]

By the time Benteen's and Reno's commands were united on Reno Hill, it was a little after 4:00 P.M. The situation on the hill can be quickly summarized. Benteen's battalion of 115 officers and men was unscathed. Reno's command had some 35 men killed and missing and 11 wounded, not all of whom were incapacitated. This left him with at least 105 effective fighters. Benteen ordered his men to divide their ammunition with Reno's. Since Reno's men, although low in ammunition, had by no means run out of it, the result was that every able-bodied trooper had more than half of his normal ration of ammunition after the transfer. The hostile fire directed toward the forces on the hill had slackened even before Benteen's approach had become obvious, and by a little after 4:00 it was virtually nonexistent. In fact, there were only a few warriors to be seen within 1,000 yards of the top of the hill.[36]

And now something strange happened. Or, to put it more precisely, the something strange was that nothing happened. Firing began to be heard downstream, and yet Reno and Benteen stood still.[37] Benteen's failure to react is probably the more noteworthy. His was certainly the dominant personality. He was seasoned in Indian warfare. His horses were tired, but they had been watered; they had not been moving quickly, and, as later events proved, they were not exhausted. His command was intact and unharmed. Above all, he was still under direct written orders to go to Custer. Yet he did not move, but in effect placed himself under Reno's command. As for Reno, he had been badly scared, and, largely due to his own precipitate actions, his command had suffered heavy losses. Yet two-thirds of his battalion was intact, and he now had ammunition and reinforcements. In the Civil War he had been in actions with similarly heavy casualties. Yet now he did not move.

It is clear that the firing downstream was audible on the hill. It is true that three years later, at the Reno court of inquiry, both Reno and Benteen said under oath that they had heard no shots then from the direction of the Custer battlefield, but the testimony seems incredible. Sgt. F. A. Culbertson said at the time to Lieutenant Varnum that he heard it, and Varnum said something to the effect that Custer must be in a serious engagement. More significantly, Lieutenant Godfrey heard it and said so to Lt. Luther Hare, who then heard it himself. Godfrey was somewhat hard of hearing; if he heard the firing, everyone else probably was physically capable of hearing it also. From the perspective of the years, it seems clear that Reno was stalling and that Benteen acquiesced. (This is not to say that they knew or consciously suspected the desperateness of Custer's situation.) Reno said that they must wait for the arrival of the pack train. In the meantime, he led a little expedition to the riverbank to recover the body of Lieutenant Hodgson, who had been killed in the retreat. By about 4:45 this mission was accomplished. The pack train had not arrived, and Reno sent Lieutenant Hare back along the trail to expedite its movement.[38]

Captain Weir, who about two hours earlier had urged Benteen to move more rapidly toward the probable scene of action, now again became uneasy at the inactivity. His lieutenant, W. S. Edgerly, fully agreed that something ought to be done. Weir went to Reno, requesting permission to move D Company downstream, "toward the sound of the guns." Reno refused, and Weir then decided to ride ahead alone to survey the situation. (Weir's, Reno's, and Hare's missions were all accomplished without mishap, which indicates how quiet the situation was at this time in the immediate vicinity of Reno Hill.) Edgerly, who had remained with D Company, saw Weir ride northward; assuming that permission had been granted, he moved the company in a direction parallel with Weir's course, although at a lower elevation. Weir rode on for about one-and-one-half miles, reaching a promontory (now called Weir's Point) from which a good view could be had of a portion of the battlefield as well as some of the intervening ridges and ravines. His survey would have been more extensive but for the fact that a pall of smoke and dust obscured his vision. He could see Indians riding about and shooting at objects on the ground. He could also see a large body of the hostiles moving toward Edgerly and D Company, and he managed to signal to his lieutenant to bring the company up to the high ground on which he stood. Edgerly did this, and D Company arrived at Weir Point about 5:30 P.M.[39]

At the same time, the pack mules carrying the extra ammunition reached Reno Hill. Ammunition was distributed until every trooper had the standard amount, but Reno still delayed his advance. The major later gave as his reason the need of obtaining blankets from the train to form litters to carry the wounded, but since at this time no Indians were as close to the top of Reno Hill as the powerful guard of the pack train, his excuse must be considered a rationalization. The entire train had reached the hilltop by about 6:00 P.M. Captain McDougall had mentioned hearing sounds of a battle downriver to Reno, who did not comment on the remark. Shortly afterward, however, the command did begin moving in the direction of Weir Point. When it reached it, the air was still laden with smoke and dust, but there was little or no sound of firing.[40] Benteen planted a company guidon somewhat in advance of Weir's station in an attempt to signal the troops' location to Custer.

Shortly afterward the Indians moved up toward the Reno-Benteen command, which was forced back to its position on Reno Hill. The battle continued until darkness came. During the night the troops made efforts at entrenchment, digging feverishly with the few tools the men possessed and even using knives and spoons. At dawn the Indian attack was renewed, and the command was hard pressed during most of the day. Benteen was the dominant spirit, and the men, including Reno himself, took heart from his courage. In midafternoon the attack slackened as the hostiles gradually withdrew. In late afternoon the exhausted command saw the whole village move up the valley in an orderly fashion.[41] It was not until midmorning of the following day that it was understood that the village had moved in response to Terry's and Gibbon's advance from the north.

The story of Reno and Benteen and their commands is known in considerable detail and with reasonable accuracy. The story of Custer's Last Stand can never be comparably well known, since there were almost certainly no military survivors,[42] and the accounts of the Crow scouts and of the hostiles show some disagreement, not only of one group with the other but even within groups. On the other hand, the testimony eventually obtained from the Indians is massive, and there are certain points of congruence. There is the testimony of Sergeant Kanipe and Trumpeter Martin, the last members of the regiment to see Custer and his command alive. There are inferences to be drawn from the observations of Benteen's and Reno's commands. Above all, perhaps, there are observations to be drawn from studies of the battlefield, beginning with those of Terry and his officers on 27 June 1876 and continuing to the present day. What follows is an attempt to synthesize this evidence, and it inevitably involves estimates as to the reliability of its various components.

We return now to 2:15 of the afternoon of 25 June, to the point just below the Lone Warrior Tepee and about two-and-one-half miles from the Little Big Horn, from which Custer sent Reno's battalion on its mission to pursue and engage the Indians on the far side of the river. After the order had been given, and as the battalion was riding off, Lieutenant Varnum rode up to Custer with a fresh report. He had been to an elevation somewhat closer to the river from which he could see a good way down the valley, and he told Custer that he had seen warriors there in considerable numbers and, beyond them to the north, a portion of what must be a very large village. Custer moved his command down the trail, not quickening the pace (he was evidently thinking over the new information) and then turned to the right. He paused for about ten minutes to water his horses at a small tributary of Reno Creek.[43] It was at about this time that Lieutenant Cooke and Captain Keogh rejoined Custer's command with the further news that the Indians were moving up the valley against Reno's battalion. Custer responded by riding to the nearest high bluff from which he could get a view of events. What he must have seen was Reno charging down the valley and a large number of Indians moving up to meet him. He could also see a large part of the Indian village strung out along the river. The time would have been shortly after 3:00 P.M. Custer may have realized that his order to Reno could turn out to have been a serious mistake. He watched until he saw Reno dismount his battalion and deploy the men as skirmishers, and from the bluff he waved his hat in encouragement.[44]

Why Custer did not now recall Reno is an incompletely answered question. Custer was not under fire, and the trail all the way back to the pack train was clear of hostiles. He could have moved to a position on or near Reno Hill, brought up Benteen and the train, and sent a company or two to Reno to help him organize a swift retreat to the bluffs. Since Reno, with little more than half the regiment, did in fact later hold out there until Terry and Gibbon arrived, there is no doubt that Custer could have done the same, meanwhile inflicting heavy casualties on the Indians, who were demonstrably in no mood for running away. In the event, Custer descended from the bluff and then sent Sergeant Kanipe back to the pack train with the message to hurry forward. He led the command farther north, using a sheltered ravine which passes by Weir Point. Here he probably halted again and rode to the crest with Tom Custer and Trumpeter Martin, his orderly for the day.[45] From this second lookout, Custer could see the village in its entirety and, perhaps for the first time, knew fully what the regiment was up against. He returned quickly to his immediate command.

The ravine along which Custer had been traveling veers at this point to the right, away from the river, and opens into Medicine Trail Coulee, a V-shaped valley, the tip of which merges with the Little Big Horn valley itself. Here the river banks are low and the water relatively shallow, making an excellent crossing place which since the time of the battle has been called the Minneconjou Ford after the Sioux tribe whose encampment was situated there. Custer led his command a short distance, perhaps 300 yards, down the near (south) fork of the coulee and then halted. It was there that he gave verbal orders to Martin to transmit to Benteen. Martin, a recent Italian immigrant (originally Giovanni Martini), had a poor command of English, and it was probably for this reason that Cooke, the adjutant, wrote the orders on a sheet from his notebook. (It is thought by Kuhlman and Gray that undoubtedly the verbal orders called specifically for *ammunition* packs, and that the key adjective was lost in the hurried transcription.) Martin was sent on his way at about 3:00 P.M., just when the attack on Reno was becoming serious.[46] As he was moving off, he saw some Sioux warriors appear from behind boulders and undergrowth and, as he thought, begin to attack Custer's column.[47] The battalion was not deterred by this, and Martin rode away believing that the Indians were being defeated. Evidently this was not yet an attack, but merely an attempt to stampede Custer's horses.

The attack in deadly earnest was soon to come. As Custer moved down Medicine Trail Coulee to hit the village in support of Reno, he was assaulted by a horde of Indians who had lain in hiding. The attack, in this phase chiefly by Sioux warriors, was so sudden and intense that the command was driven to the high ground to the northeast, the area now called the Custer Battlefield. Keogh (I Company) and Calhoun (L Company) appear to have formed a sort of rear guard holding off the Indian onslaught and permitting a moderately strong defensive position to be formed higher on the ridge. The core of the command appears to have been moving northeasterly when it was checked from the rear by a strong body of Indians made up of Cheyenne and Sioux under Crazy Horse and Two Moon.[48] The assault from the south and west now grew stronger as many Indians, released from fighting in the valley to the south when Reno retreated, came down to join those who had first forced Custer away from Medicine Trail Coulee. These Indians were led by the valiant Gall of the Huncpapas, who had been the principal war chief in the fight against Reno.[49] Pressed on all sides, and by this time greatly diminished in numbers, most of the remaining troopers (seemingly about forty) gathered about Custer and the regimental standard and formed a defensive nucleus high on the ridge, about where the Custer Monument now stands. The troopers shot their horses and used them as breastworks. Crouching behind the bodies and firing at close range, the little band held out some time.

How long did the command survive? It is impossible to say with any assurance. Weir and Edgerly probably were unable to see the whole battlefield through the smoke and dust. Their observations seem to have been confined to the portions where Calhoun's and Keogh's companies lay fallen with the Indians shooting into their bodies. The Indian accounts vary widely, some maintaining that this whole phase of the battle took less than an hour and others supporting the belief that it was a matter of several hours. However, the logic of the situation, based on the nature of the terrain and the Indians' manner of fighting, suggests that the longer estimates are closer to the truth. Reno's command did not reach the hill until close to 4:00 P.M. Only then were the Indians under Chief Gall released to ride to the north and join in the attack on Custer. Until about 4:30, then, Custer's situation was grave but not hopeless. He had lost many men, perhaps three-fourths of Keogh's and Calhoun's companies and a few men from the other three companies. Yet he had with him, until Gall's onslaught, about 150 men. He was hemmed in, but the men were fighting for their lives under the direction of seasoned officers. Then, when the final defense nucleus was formed, it would have been still more costly to assail.

Moreover, one must take into account the Indian way of fighting. The Sioux and Cheyenne had, in the Custer fight, a number of truly outstanding leaders who had proven their mettle in many an encounter with the whites: Gall, Crazy Horse, Crow King, and Low Dog of the Sioux; and Two Moon, Wooden Leg, and others of the Cheyenne. And yet there were no organized formations; these chiefs could not issue specific, let alone complex, orders. They led by example and exhortation. As light cavalrymen, the Indians individually were superb, but their military and social structure did not permit the kind of organized charge in which heavy losses are routinely accepted for a specified objective. Until the very last moments of the Custer fight, when a wave of mounted warriors swept over the few remaining troopers, there is every reason to believe that the Indians fought dismounted, creeping forward and taking every advantage of such meager cover as the terrain afforded.

There has been a great deal of discussion as to the nature of the weapons available to the Indians in the Battle of the Little Big Horn, a discussion that began in the immediate aftermath of the debacle. It was natural enough for the army to seek to fix the blame on factors other than those of strategy, tactics, and leadership. Even Colonel Graham's scholarly study maintains that the Indians were better armed than the troopers of the Seventh Cavalry; the blame is placed upon unscrupulous traders at the various reservations who sold repeating rifles to the Indians, whereas the troopers carried single-shot carbines.[50] There is no question that some of the hostiles were thus equipped, but evidence strongly suggests that they were a decided minority. (When, for example, in the years immediately following the battle, driven by hunger and pursued by ever-increasing numbers of soldiers, the Indians came in to the reservations to surrender, they had relatively few repeating rifles.) It appears that the Indians at the Battle of the Little Big Horn were armed with all sorts of firearms, from Spencer repeaters to ancient muzzle-loaders, and, furthermore, that many of them had no firearms at all, relying on bows and arrows, clubs and hatchets.[51]

This point about the Indians' weapons is critical in estimating the duration of the Last Stand. Given a rough equality of armament, it is scarcely credible that a generally seasoned body of troopers, fighting for their lives with the regimental commander and not having to face an organized charge, would have been silenced in an hour or so by an enemy who was under no time pressure. It seems more likely that the fight lasted about two hours, or until about 5:30. Apparently, then, the last of Custer's little band succumbed shortly before Reno began his movement toward the battlefield.

FIVE

Questions Raised by Custer's Behavior

APART from some queries in the press in the immediate aftermath of the Battle of the Little Big Horn, the question of why Terry's forces did not produce a victory has seldom been raised seriously. It is true that Colonel Gibbon, on 6 November 1876, wrote to Terry:

> So great was my fear that Custer's zeal would carry him forward too rapidly that the last thing I said to him when bidding him good bye after his regiment had filed past you when starting on his march was, "Now Custer, don't be greedy, but wait for us." He replied gaily, as with a wave of his hand he dashed off to follow his regiment, "No, I will not." Poor fellow! Knowing what we do now, and what an effect a fresh Indian trail seemed to have had upon him, perhaps we were expecting too much to anticipate a forbearance on his part which would have rendered cooperation of the two columns practicable.
>
> Except so far as to draw profit from past experience it is perhaps useless to speculate as to what would have been the result had your plan, as originally agreed upon, been carried out. But I cannot help reflecting that in that case, my column, supposing the Indian camp to have remained where it was when Custer first struck it, would have been the first to reach it, that with our infantry and Gatling guns we should have been able to take care of ourselves, even though numbering only about two-thirds of Custer's force, and that with 600 cavalry in the neighborhood, led as only Custer would lead it, the result to the Indians would have been very different from what it was.[1]

In commenting upon this letter years later, Col. Robert P. Hughes, Terry's aide-de-camp at the time of the battle, added:

> The remainder of Custer's column was able to hold out against the victory flushed Indians until Terry and Gibbon came up. Then, notwithstanding the fact that this latter force numbered but 400 men, and the Indian force was practically untouched, they incontinently fled. Is it not easily conceivable that, had Gibbon and Custer been acting together, as Terry had planned, the force would certainly have had no "check", much less an overwhelming disaster, if indeed it failed of a signal victory?[2]

As a matter of fact, the Indian force was not "practically untouched," although it was indeed still very strong. It had almost certainly suffered a good many casualties which could not be counted by the whites, since the retreating Indians took their dead and wounded with them. Moreover, the Indians, while they had acquired some additional firearms during the fight, had very little ammunition and were unable to acquire more. Gibbon and Hughes wrote their comments to explain a disastrous campaign, but they still cannot be taken lightly. Both were men of integrity, and Gibbon, in particular, was an experienced officer. Yet such evaluations and the few others like them involve a glossing over of important elements of the situation. Given the large number of hostile Indians (an average of informed estimates has placed this at about 3,000, but John S. Gray's reliable study places it at 1,780 exclusive of young boys and old men; possibly the total was about 2,000);[3] given the presence of inspiring leaders such as Gall, Crazy Horse, Crow King, and Two Moon; given the Indians' knowledge that forces were in the field against them and in their vicinity; given the roughness of the terrain; and given the high mobility of the Indians, it would have required a certain amount of good luck plus near-perfect execution of Terry's rather clumsy plan to have avoided some measure of defeat, let alone to have produced a victory.

If Custer had started later or moved more slowly, and if the Indians had heavily engaged the Terry-Gibbon column a short distance from the mouth of the Little Big Horn and were prepared to fight a delaying action there, and if, while they were so engaged, Custer had swept down the Little Big Horn valley with his whole command, things might indeed have turned out differently, and there might even have been a victory for the military. Such an eventuality would, however, have involved a series of improbabilities, the chief of which is that the Indians would have held still for that type of fight.

The principal and enduring questions do not have to do with the reasons Terry or Custer did not produce a victory, but rather with the reasons for Custer's having become involved in a defeat so severe that it involved the annihilation of his personal command, five companies of cavalry, and the crippling of the rest of the regiment. In the history of Little Big Horn and Custer studies it was naturally the case that the first questions raised had to do with strategic and tactical decisions at a purely conscious level. As the study of the campaign continued, however, it became apparent to at least some students that an attempt at understanding could not stop with conscious, logical considerations. Thus, for example, Fred Dustin has suggested in *The Custer Tragedy* that features of Custer's temperament were appreciably important in determining his course of action. Edgar I. Stewart, in *Custer's Luck*, has occasionally argued that a decision of Custer's could only be understood or deduced by taking into consideration certain deep-seated and not entirely conscious personality features. Thus straightforward questions of conscious military judgment have come to be blended with questions having to do with subtle, partly unconscious aspects of personality: Custer's personality and the personalities of his superior, Terry, and his principal subordinates.

The present work focuses on Custer's personality and the effects of this personality upon the fight at the Little Big Horn. I certainly do not mean to imply that the personalities and personal conflicts of other key figures are irrelevant to the battle and its outcome, or that psychological features, however interesting, constitute more than one aspect of many factors determining events. I do not intend, for example, to suggest that the Indians at the Little Big Horn could not have exacted fearful casualties of any leader and any command that might have been sent against them in similar force.

This having been said, what are the questions to which a careful analysis of Custer's personality may afford more complete answers than have earlier been possible? The most significant may be formulated as follows:

1. Why did Custer blurt out to Colonel Ludlow his intentions of "swinging loose from Terry"?

2. What was the meaning of the scene shortly thereafter, when he assured Terry of his loyalty?

3. Why did he, against Sherman's clear wishes, take along the reporter Mark Kellogg?

4. Why did he refuse the Gatling guns?

5. Why did he refuse one or more of Major Brisbin's four troops of cavalry?

6. Why did he not point out the defects in Terry's plan of campaign?

7. What was the significance of his change of mood during the conference aboard the *Far West?*

8. Why did he urge on his command the taking of provisions for an expedition of perhaps considerably longer than fifteen days, when it was clear that Terry, however naively, had in mind some sort of combined operation?

9. Why did he address his officers in a highly uncharacteristic manner on 22 June?

10. Why did he persist, in the face of repeated warnings from his scouts, in underestimating the number of hostile Indians?

11. Why did he not explore Tulloch's Creek as he had been specifically ordered to do?

12. Why did he not send Scout Herendeen to Terry, as Terry had ordered and expected?

13. Why did he not continue south, as Terry had clearly suggested, particularly inasmuch as conditions were no different from those Terry had anticipated in his letter of instructions?

14. Why did he order the rapid march of 24 June, and especially the noisy night advance, when the command was already fully on schedule or even ahead of it?

15. Why, in view of his good strategic position on the Rosebud side of the divide, did he not rest his command and perform a proper reconnaisance?

16. Why was he ambiguous about believing the scouts' report of what they had seen in the early morning of 25 June from the Crow's Nest?

17. Why did he divide his command into four fractions just prior to his probable attack, even though he must have known he was greatly outnumbered?

18. Why did he send Benteen on the fruitless "scout to the left"?

19. Why did he not summon Reno back when he saw his plight?

20. Why did he not fall back upon Benteen, the pack train, and Reno when he saw the immense size of the Indian village?

Other students have offered specific answers, at least partially adequate, to many of these specific questions. Sometimes these answers have been detailed. However, they are not entirely convincing, and indeed sometimes they have been conflicting. There is at least a faint suggestion that some basic underlying theme is being hidden by the very multiplicity of details. Let me, then, tentatively identify the most basic question. What was interfering with Custer's personal effectiveness? That is, what was preventing him from functioning smoothly, from making better decisions, from exercising his full capabilities? What was leading him to move headlong into a doomed situation?

One can only approach this complex problem by considering Custer's personal history, an interesting story in itself.

Major General George Armstrong Custer. Ca. 1865.

Emanuel H. Custer, Custer's father. Photo by C. W. Hill, Monroe, Michigan, ca. 1865.

Maria Ward Kirkpatrick Custer, Custer's mother. Photo by C. W. Hill, Monroe Michigan.

Elizabeth Bacon Custer. Ca. 1876.

Custer and Elizabeth Custer during a meal in camp. Ca. 1867.

Custer, Thomas Ward Custer, and Elizabeth Custer. Ca. 1865.

Thomas Ward Custer, Custer's brother. Ca. 1864.

Custer and Maggie Custer Calhoun during charades at Fort Abraham Lincoln. Ca. 1875.

Captain Frederick Benteen.

Major Marcus A. Reno. *Smithsonian Institution Photo No. 65–A–2.*

Sitting Bull of the Sioux. Photo by D. F. Barry, Bismarck, Dakota Territory, ca. 1885.

Gall of the Sioux. Photo by D. F. Barry, ca. 1880.

Two Moon of the Cheyenne. Photo by L. A. Huffman, 1878.

Curly, one of Custer's Crow scouts. Ca. 1876.

SIX

Custer's Early Years

GEORGE ARMSTRONG CUSTER was born to Emanuel Henry and his second wife, Maria W. K. Custer, in the hamlet of New Rumley, Ohio, on 5 December 1839. Emanuel, like his father before him, was a blacksmith; he was thirty-two when George was born. He had migrated to Ohio from Maryland some twelve years earlier. Emanuel was a third-generation American, his grandfather, also named Emanuel, having come from Hesse in the Germanies around the middle of the eighteenth century. This first Emanuel had fought in the Revolutionary War—a fact proudly remembered in the family—and probably became a man of substance, since his American wife was a cousin of the mother of George Washington. But in any case, the family fortunes had slipped by the time of George's birth, for his father never prospered. He seems to have had no head for business, and, while his family was never in want, he was at times hard pressed to make ends meet.[1]

Emanuel's first wife, Matilda Viers, whom he married in 1828, died in 1834. There were three children of this union, all of whom survived their mother. Custer's mother, Maria Ward, was of English descent and was born in Burgettstown, Pennsylvania, in 1807. Married at eighteen to Israel Kirkpatrick, she bore him three (or possibly four) children during their ten years of marriage, which ended with his death in 1835. Thus Emanuel and Maria, the widower and the widow, had a ready-made family when they married on 14 April 1837. They all seem to have got on well together, but Emanuel and Maria's happiness was marred during the first two years of their marriage by the deaths in infancy of the first two children, both sons, of their union. Their third child, George Armstrong, called "Autie" by his family after his own childhood efforts to pronounce his middle name, was thus understandably the favorite of both mother and father from the moment of his birth.[2] His position among his half-siblings was obviously preeminent.

After Maria Custer's three quick pregnancies, there ensued a lull. Nevin was born on 29 July 1842, followed by Thomas in 1845, Boston in 1848, and Margaret in 1852. Nevin was a sickly child, apparently the only such in the family. Autie's favorite among his full siblings was Tom;[3] thus he followed the pattern frequent among siblings of forming a special alliance with the one born second after oneself. This affection was strongly returned; Tom became Autie's most devoted admirer and imitator.

What is known of Emanuel and Maria's personalities and characteristics helps one to understand the family climate and the influences that played upon Custer as a child. Emanuel was physically very strong, but limited in education, in business judgment, in ambition, and in means. He was extraordinarily interested in politics, about which he talked a great deal with anyone who would join in or even listen. He was an ardent Jacksonian Democrat, but here also he was not a doer.[4] There is no record of his ever having stood for office or formally campaigned for a friend. As is well attested by surviving letters to Custer and others, Emanuel was intelligent, but this intelligence seems never to have been harnessed to any sustained purpose. As he loved to talk, he loved to sing, and it has been noted that in church his voice could be heard above all the others when a hymn was sung.

He was a practical joker, especially within his family, and his manner seems to have invited jokes upon himself in return. His relationship to his sons seems to have been more that of an elder brother than of a traditional father. The horseplay among Emanuel and the boys continued long after Autie and Tom had grown to manhood.[5] Emanuel had a liking for soldiering, although again there seems to have been an element of fantasy in his activities. He never served a hitch in the army, but he was an active member of the Ohio militia, and when it drilled during the 1840s he often would take Autie along with him.[6] The boy was quick to learn and would imitate his father's maneuvers. Emanuel was anything but a disciplinarian,[7] despite his penchant for the military, and such regulations as prevailed in the household must have been imposed by Maria.

One wishes that more were known about Maria Custer. It is certain that Autie was her favorite and that she was greatly concerned about Nevin,[8] who must have occupied more than his share of her time. It seems—although it is of course impossible to be sure—that Autie's ambitiousness came from his mother. It also appears that Maria, with her British background, was socially a shade above Emanuel. She was a woman of strong moral principles, which she endeavored to inculcate in her family.

The photographs of Emanuel and Maria Custer taken in their later years and now preserved in the Custer Battlefield Museum reveal much about the couple. Emanuel wears a sizable beard but has an almost unlined forehead. He has a large mouth, with the corners of the lips drawn down slightly in a somewhat wry expression. Maria Custer must have been an attractive woman in her youth, for her face is still handsome. She has a firm chin, expressive of determination. Her forehead is somewhat lined, and she wears genteel little spectacles. Her appearance is highly intelligent, and, although she is faintly smiling (no doubt for the photographer), the downward folds at the corners of her lips are pronounced, suggesting that her finely chiseled features may have assumed a sterner expression at times.

There is one other set of features about Maria Custer which can only be documented from her later life, and whose influence or even existence during Autie's formative years is only a conjecture. Although she lived to seventy-five,

Maria was considered to be ill for many of these years. In fact, she behaved like a partial invalid for at least the last decade of her life and probably longer. The nature of her illness is obscure, but whatever it was, a large "secondary gain" element seems to have gone with it; that is to say, it won for Maria a large share of the family's sympathies and attention. Although her hold over Autie had other and deeper roots, this element came to play a part in it. Elizabeth Custer gives a vivid picture of this aspect of the mother-son relationship, and it was one which can only be called selfish on the mother's part.

> The hardest trial of my husband's life was parting with his mother. Such partings were the only occasions when I ever saw him lose entire control of himself. . . . She had been an invalid for so many years that each parting seemed to her the final one. Her groans and sobs were heartrending. She clung to him every step when he started to go, and exhausted at last was led back, half-fainting, to her lounge. . . . The general would rush out of the house, sobbing like a child, and then throw himself into the carriage beside me, completely unnerved. . . . At the first stop he was out of the car in an instant, buying fresh fruit to send back to her. Before we were even unpacked in the hotel, where we had made our first stay of any length, he had dashed off a letter.[9]

A number of anecdotes have been preserved of Custer's childhood and youth, of which the one perhaps most often quoted has to do with a trip to the dentist at age four. He had had a severe toothache and had been taken by his father to the dentist in the little town of Scio, two or three miles from New Rumley. The tooth had been pulled and little Autie had been very brave. Walking along the street in Scio, he turned to look up at his father and said, "Father, you and me can whip all the Whigs in Ohio!"[10] Whether the dentist was a Whig has not been passed on, but in any case the remark is of interest as indicating a special way of dealing with anxiety and pain.

As has been mentioned, there was a certain military coloring to Autie's early life, since Emanuel drilled with the local militia during the Mexican war. When still quite small, Autie surprised the family one day by declaiming a climactic line from Addison's *Cato* (which was being committed to memory by an older half-brother): "My voice is still for war!"[11]

Although anecdotes such as these clearly indicate aggression in Autie's nature, there is no evidence that the aggression often got out of hand. Autie was an active, hardy, and athletic boy, but he was good-natured, never bullying or mean, and usually in the thick of whatever fun was going on. He was competitive and wanted to excel in boyish pursuits; he usually did excel, except in school.[12] He was undoubtedly intelligent, but he was a careless and undisciplined student, getting by, one supposes, by applying himself only when it was necessary.

When Autie was still quite small—the year seems to have been 1842—the Custers moved for a short time to the outskirts of Monroe, Michigan, a place that was to become permanently identified with the family. Emanuel rented a small farm, but as usual his business fortunes were not good. The family was forced to return to New Rumley after about six months, but during their brief stay in

Michigan Lydia Ann Custer met David Reed, who lived on a neighboring farm, and was much attracted to him. Not long afterward David came to New Rumley, carried on a whirlwind courtship, and married Lydia Ann. He took her back with him to Monroe, where he established himself in the draying business.

When Autie was nine, he was apprenticed to a cabinetmaker in Cadiz, the county seat of Harrison County, in which New Rumley and Scio are located. The motives for this arrangement are unclear; possibly it was a reaction to his mediocre performance at school. Whatever the reasons, the experiment did not work out. In 1840, ten-year-old Autie was sent to live with his sister Lydia in Monroe. Lydia seems to have been much like her mother, and indeed she was a second mother to Autie. She was a religious woman, fundamentalist in tendencies, strict about behavior, and sympathetic to—perhaps even stimulating of—ambitions in her younger brother. There was no more talk of his becoming an artisan. Although still an erratic student, Autie went to a good school in Monroe (Alfred Stebbins's Young Men's Academy), and when he returned to Ohio several years later he continued his education.[13]

The situation in Monroe seems likely to have made an alert young person such as Autie conscious of social stratification. This town, although the population totaled only 3,500, was relatively cosmopolitan compared to New Rumley or Scio. The community was composed largely of three ethnic groups: British, French, and German. Those of British derivation were at the top of the social ladder. The social distinctions were reflected in the places of worship. The French were Catholic and therefore somewhat a special case. Most of the citizens of British ancestry worshiped at the Presbyterian church, while those folk of humbler origins, including most of the settlers of German derivation, worshiped at the Methodist church. It is an interesting sociological point that the Custers attended the Methodist church when they were in Monroe, feeling more at home there, whereas in Ohio they had gone to Scio to attend the Presbyterian church.[14]

There is a strong family tradition that Autie met his future wife, Elizabeth ("Libbie") Bacon, during his first stay in Monroe. The meeting was brief and informal, and it clearly crossed the lines of social stratification. Autie was so active and energetic that he must have caught Libbie's eye before their first encounter, for she knew who he was. The story goes that as Autie was coming home from school one day, Libbie was swinging on the front gate of the substantial Bacon home. She took the initiative momentarily, saying, "Hello, you Custer boy!" What Autie said in response has not been passed down, but there was no real conversation, for Libbie's courage did not sustain her; she ran into the house.[15] If one may judge by pictures of her taken a few years later, Libbie was rightly considered the prettiest young lady in Monroe, and she must have been a charming little girl. Certainly Autie did not forget her.

Libbie's father, Daniel S. Bacon, was a power in Monroe and a well-known and respected figure in the state. Born in Saratoga, New York, of English stock, rather well educated although not wealthy, Bacon had migrated to Monroe as a young man. He taught school at first, but acquired property and became interested in public affairs. In 1835 he was elected to the Legislative Council of the Territory of Michigan, and in 1845 he was elected to the state legislature. He became a judge of probate in Monroe, a position he retained for some years. When he was just past forty, Bacon met and married Eleanor Page, who was originally from Vermont. Libbie, born in 1842, was their only child. She lost her mother when she was ten. Judge Bacon remarried, and the relationship between Libbie and her stepmother seems to have been good. Libbie attended Boyd's Seminary, did very well, and was valedictorian of her class. During her growing-up years, there was only the most distant contact between Libbie and Autie. Much later, a member of the Bacons' circle expressed the sense of social distance by saying, "We did not associate with [the Reeds and Custers]; they were quite ordinary people, no intellectual interests, very little schooling."[16]

It seems possible that such sociological considerations exerted an effect upon Autie, adding to the ambitiousness already rooted in parental (particularly his mother's) expectations. However, his life was full and active and occupied with other matters. After returning to Ohio, he continued to visit Monroe occasionally, and he had many friends in both places. He was popular with his associates, both boys and girls, being always ready for a good time and the leader in many a youthful prank. Autie's engaging manner made it relatively easy for him to be the center of attention, a situation which he relished. He was clever and could usually arrange things to get what he wanted. Jay Monaghan relates a rollicking little adventure which sounds as though it might have been typical.

> In Monroe, Armstrong began going with girls. Soon he was playing the field in both Michigan and Ohio. Girls liked the smiling curlyhead. He had traveled more than his comrades and a date with Autie was exciting. He kept the crowd laughing, was usually planning a practical joke, and his friends never knew what was going to happen next. For example, once on a bright winter day at New Rumley, he and Joe Dickenson decided to take the neighborhood belles sleighriding in a straw-filled wagon box on runners. They packed the girls in under buffalo robes where it was warm, cozy, and lots of fun. But Autie kept reminding Joe about another lass on the next farm and the team jingled over the snowy roads to stop at her kitchen door. Finally so many girls were packed in the sleigh that Joe had to ride one of the horses. Out in the cold, he concluded that Autie had planned this prank from the beginning as a joke on him. Joe decided to get even. He whipped the team along the road and at the first sharp turn rolled the laughing load into a big drift. Armstrong was somewhere at the bottom of that screaming, squealing, melee of rosy cheeks, kicking legs, and flying snow. More noticeable still, he took what seemed to Joe an unnecessarily long time to surface. Watching from above, Joe decided that instead of "jobbing" Armstrong, Armstrong had "jobbed" him.[17]

Impulsiveness and a vulnerability to slights and depreciatory remarks (of which, at this stage, he did not encounter many) also were characteristics of Autie's, as is shown in the following incident, preserved by family tradition and related by Monaghan, Van de Water, and others. While Autie was taking part in a spelling bee at school in his late teens, one of the other students attempted to upset his concentration by making faces at him from outside the window. Without hesitating, Autie smashed his fist through the window, hitting the offender in the nose.[18]

As has been noted, Custer excelled in athletics of many sorts; having grown up largely on a farm, he quickly learned to ride and became a good horseman long before his army training. It has been reported, however, that he did not participate in swimming or boating and that, in fact, he had an "odd fear of the water."[19] This phobia must have been mild, for he liked fishing and, on one important occasion during the Civil War, waded the Chickahominy River. Yet the point is not without psychological interest, and it fits in with other aspects of Custer's personality yet to be discussed.

Custer finished high school in Harrison County, and it seems to have been at about this time that the idea of going to West Point and having a military career, which he had thought of tentatively for some time, took a firm grasp on his imagination. While working on this plan, he took some further courses at McNeely Normal School in Hopedale, Ohio, and then served for about nine months as principal of a small school on the outskirts of Athens, Ohio, some ninety miles to the southeast of Scio and New Rumley. In order to reach West Point, he had somehow to get the necessary recommendation from a member of Congress. Custer's family had little influence of any kind; moreover, John A. Bingham, the representative from their home district, was a Whig, whereas the Custers were Democrats. However, young Custer wrote Bingham a remarkable letter, disarming in its frankness and persuasive in its picture of himself. He mentioned the family's political leanings, said that he felt sure that partisan considerations would not influence Bingham, and described himself in favorable terms, including, among other assets, that he was "of above the medium height and of remarkably strong construction and vigorous frame." Bingham later claimed to have been greatly impressed by the letter, and, although he had already named a man for the year Custer wished to enter, he promised to obtain an appointment for him the following year. Bingham made good his word, and Custer set off for West Point in June 1857. To raise the money for his outfitting Emanuel sold the small farm.[20]

There were entrance examinations to be taken on his arrival. Of 108 men examined, 68 passed, including Custer, and, as was the custom, he was accredited for a six-month probationary period, beginning 1 July. The details of Custer's West Point experiences have been told in Frederick Whittaker's *Complete Life of General George A. Custer,* Frederick W. Van de Water's *Glory-Hunter,* Lawrence A. Frost's *Custer Album,* and Jay Monaghan's *Custer,* and the points of psychological interest may be easily summarized.

1. Custer made many friends and enjoyed socializing when he was off duty. His friendships were largely with cadets from the southern and western states; he associated less readily with the more sophisticated and generally better-educated eastern boys.

2. In his studies he barely got by, almost certainly because he lacked intellectual discipline and had a shaky educational foundation, and not because he lacked native intelligence. The subject which, by his own later admission, meant the least to him was philosophy.

3. Custer's most serious difficulties were caused by his deportment. Cadets were given demerits for all sorts of infractions of the strict regulations. One hundred demerits in any given half-year meant automatic expulsion, and Custer regularly accumulated more than ninety. The demerits were not given for behavior which was malign or underhanded. They were virtually all given for such relatively minor offenses as failing to have a neat appearance on parade, having an untidy room, taking inadequate care of equipment, having food in his room, being tardy for classes, and being late for morning report. Custer's deportment did not improve during his four years at West Point; in his last half-year he received ninety-seven demerits.[21]

4. Most of the cadets acquired nicknames while at West Point. Custer was called by at least three: "Fanny," "Cinnamon," and "Curly." The latter two were derived respectively from Custer's fashion of wearing his reddish-blond hair unusually long and from his using a cinnamon preparation as a hairdressing. The origin of the first nickname is unknown.[22]

More important than any of these various difficulties and eccentricities is the basic fact that Custer, coming from humble origins and with certain educational disadvantages, did finish the course.

SEVEN

The Civil War Years

ON arriving in Washington in July 1861—a few days later than the rest of his class, having been held over for a court-martial for a minor offense—Custer reported to army general headquarters. He was introduced to the chief of staff, old Gen. Winfield Scott. Perhaps because of the chaos which then prevailed, Scott offered Custer a choice of assignments. He could either join the regiment for which he had been designated, the Second Cavalry, or assist Gen. Joseph Mansfield in drilling new recruits to the volunteer army. Being eager for action, Custer chose the former and was sent to join his regiment, then commanded by a Maj. Innes Palmer as a part of David Hunter's division in Irvin McDowell's Army of the Potomac.[1] Custer thus was present on the periphery at the first Battle of Bull Run. He saw little action, but he performed a brave and useful service in preventing the retreat in his immediate sector at Cub Run from becoming as much of a rout as was the case in most of the Union army on that day. In fact, G Company (Custer's) was the last unit to leave the battlefield.[2] Custer was mentioned for bravery in the report of his division.

In the reorganization which followed Bull Run, Custer was assigned as an aide to Brig. Gen. Philip Kearny, who then commanded a brigade of four regiments of New Jersey volunteers. This assignment was brief and militarily uneventful, but it is of some psychological interest. It was the first of a series of assignments to forceful and competent general officers, and, like the others, it was carried out in a faithful and highly satisfactory manner. Kearny was older than most officers of his rank; he was wealthy, a superb combat leader, and a rigid disciplinarian. He undoubtedly made a considerable impression on the hitherto undisciplined Custer.[3] In fact, some process of identification may well have taken place, for, when he was given commands of his own, Custer tended to behave more like Kearny than like any other officer with whom he had had close working contact.

In October 1861, Custer was given a sick leave for unknown reasons and returned to Monroe. There an incident occurred which was to have a temporary effect upon his fortunes and a lasting effect upon his behavior. He became drunk in a tavern with some old school friends. Clowning and weaving his way to his sister's home, he passed Libbie's house and was seen by that young lady in his unsteady state, a misfortune which considerably slowed the process of their becoming acquainted. Once he arrived at Lydia's, his sister took one look at him, picked up the family Bible, and led him aside for a lecture on temperance. Whether it was his sister's eloquence, the image of Libbie looking at him from her window, or both that exerted a profound effect upon Custer cannot be known, but the fact is that he never drank again.[4]

In the spring of 1862, during Gen. George McClellan's Peninsular Campaign, Custer, nominally assigned to the Fifth Cavalry, was placed on detached duty. He served briefly as a balloonist-observer, reporting on the position of Confederate formations.[5] On 5 May, the combination of Custer's courage and the good luck which was frequently to be his during the Civil War brought him an outstanding success. With no authorization, he had gone along with Brig. Gen. Winfield S. Hancock, whose brigade was soon being very severely pressed by the enemy. Hancock had formed his line to meet the Confederate advance, and, at the point of greatest pressure, he ordered one of his units to charge.

> The men started forward, hesitantly. They believed themselves outnumbered and trapped. Then, from their wavering ranks, rode an unkempt figure, Custer. At first they thought he was a threadbare newspaper correspondent, in a discarded military jacket, who had ventured out on the firing line for a story. The fellow's long hair hung over his collar. He waved a tattered hat, shouted gleefully, and urged them all forward. Cowards felt brave when they saw Armstrong's laughing, freckled face. If bullets failed to hit him up there on a horse, men on the ground should be safe. They all began to cheer and run forward.
>
> The enemy hesitated before the blue infantry wave with its tossing foam of bayonets. For a moment the gray line stood, then broke and retreated, abandoning the bastion and leaving a battle flag behind, the first captured by the Army of the Potomac.[6]

For this daring and unconventional act of leadership, Hancock gave Custer a citation for bravery.

On 22 May there was a similar occurrence, which brought Custer to the attention of the commanding general of the Army of the Potomac, George McClellan. Again personal bravery and good fortune were combined. McClellan was planning a crossing of the Chickahominy River toward Richmond. He had ordered his chief of engineers, Brig. Gen. John G. Barnard, to reconnoiter the river. By chance Barnard came upon Custer and ordered him to wade into the Chickahominy and determine whether it could be forded by infantry at a certain point. Custer performed this task promptly, effectively, and with a series of pertinent observations. As a result, McClellan offered him a position on his staff and the temporary rank of captain with it. Custer at once accepted.[7] At just about the same time, he was also promoted on the permanent army list to the rank of first lieutenant, nominally assigned to the Fifth Cavalry. Custer got on with McClellan extremely well, as he usually did with any superior officer ranking far above him. When McClellan was replaced as commanding general by Ambrose Burnside, he retained Custer on his staff. Custer had, however, no immediate duties, so he was given a leave of absence and returned to Monroe.

It was during this visit that Custer was formally introduced to Libbie Bacon. They met several times, and despite Libbie's early standoffishness because of the intoxication episode, there was a strong mutual attraction. Judge Bacon, however, asked his daughter to discontinue receiving Captain Custer, for he did not consider the young man socially acceptable. Nonetheless, Armstrong and Libbie continued meeting at parties, and when the leave was at an end they arranged to keep in touch through one of Libbie's girlfriends.[8]

From February to mid-April of 1863, Custer assisted McClellan in preparing his final report of the Peninsular Campaign, and he was then ordered to rejoin his regiment, reverting to the rank of lieutenant. At this time Maj. Gen. Alfred Pleasonton was chief of cavalry of the Army of the Potomac. Custer's previous service with Kearny and McClellan was probably the basis for Pleasonton's appointing him as aide in June. He was effective in this capacity, being of particular service to Pleasonton in keeping him informed of enemy movement. Custer kept up the pattern of being the right man in the right place at the right time. In an engagement at Aldie, Virginia, on 16 June, two Union cavalry regiments were being worsted by one of J. E. B. Stuart's brigades; their colonels were vainly attempting to organize a rally. Whittaker describes what then happened.

> So great was the turmoil that neither colonel could be heard, when forth from the crowd rode a third figure, a young captain, wearing a broad plantation hat, from under which long bright curls attracted attention wherever he went. Out he rode beside Kilpatrick and Douty, waved his long blade in the air, and pointed to the enemy, then turned his horse and galloped toward them. . . . He looked back and beckoned with his sword. "Come on, boys," he shouted.[9]

Colonels Kilpatrick and Douty were soon at Custer's side. Seeing their leaders advance, the troopers rushed forward. After sharp fighting, the tide was turned.

In recognition of this feat and other services, Pleasonton submitted Custer's name (along with those of three other officers) for promotion to the temporary rank of brigadier general. The appointments were made,[10] and Custer, at twenty-three, thus became the youngest general officer in the United States army since the marquis de Lafayette. He received word of the promotion on 29 June. He was in command of the Michigan Cavalry Brigade, and he had to take over and move out immediately. Robert E. Lee and the Army of Northern Virginia had crossed over into Pennsylvania, and George Gordon Meade, newly appointed commander of the Army of the Potomac, was moving to keep between Lee and Washington. The Michigan brigade formed the advance guard of Meade's army.

On 1 and 2 July, the first days of the Battle of Gettysburg, Custer and his brigade played a respectable but not remarkable role. On 3 July, however, his combat leadership played an important part in turning back a determined sweep by Stuart's cavalry, which was attempting to encircle Meade's right. Again Custer happened to be the right man on the spot. He had received orders to move his brigade to the other end of the line,[11] and, had he done so, this phase of the battle might have proved critical for the Union army. Capt. William E. Miller of the Third Pennsylvania Cavalry later gave an eyewitness account of the decisive moments.

> Gregg, meeting Custer, who was about to begin his march in the opposite direction, had ordered him to return. . . . Custer, eager for the fray, had wheeled about and was soon on the field. . . .
>
> . . . there appeared moving toward us a large mass of cavalry, which proved to be the remaining portions of Wade Hampton's and Fitzhugh Lee's brigades. They were formed in close column of squadrons and directed their course toward the Spangler House. A grander spectacle than their advance has rarely been beheld. . . . Shell and shrapnel met the advancing Confederates and tore through their ranks. Closing the gaps as though nothing had happened, on they came. . . . The 1st Michigan, drawn up in close column of squadrons near Pennington's battery, was ordered by Gregg to charge. Custer the brigade commander, who was near, placed himself at the head, and off they dashed. As the two columns approached each other the pace of each increased, when suddenly a crash like the falling of timber, betokened the crisis. So sudden and violent was the collision that many of the horses were turned end over end.[12]

Miller did not know that Custer's remaining with General Gregg was at Custer's request and was technically in violation of his immediate orders. The counter-charge was successful in stopping Stuart's brigades. This episode occurred at the same time as a more significant event—the wrecking of Pickett's charge on Cemetery Ridge. In effect, the two actions ended the battle.

At the beginning of October 1863, after some further hard but inconclusive fighting, Custer was given a well-earned leave by Pleasonton and again went to Monroe. He at once saw Libbie, and shortly afterward she agreed to marry him. There was still the matter of Judge Bacon's consent. Custer found it difficult to approach him on the subject, and the judge did not help matters. In fact, he left Monroe during Custer's stay, claiming business affairs required his presence in Traverse City, but he returned in time to join Libbie in seeing Custer off at the end of his leave. Custer said something about writing to the judge on a serious matter and departed. He postponed writing for several days, and when he did, asking for Libbie's hand, in return he received a temporizing letter from the judge. By the end of November, after some further correspondence and a good bit of coaxing of her father by Libbie, Custer received a favorable reply. The wedding was performed in the Presbyterian church in Monroe on 9 February 1864.[13]

The spring of 1864 saw two important changes in the command structure of the Union army, particularly with respect to the war in Virginia. Meade retained the immediate command of the Army of the Potomac, but Ulysses S. Grant became chief of staff, spending much of his energy supervising Meade on the spot, and Philip Sheridan became chief of cavalry. Sheridan admired Custer for his vigor and daring, and he usually placed the Michigan brigade at the head of the cavalry column in any major thrust. That year Custer saw considerable action and won further renown. In May he participated in Sheridan's raid on Richmond. On 11 May he led his brigade in an advance on a battery of J. E. B. Stuart at Yellow Tavern. The advance had culminated in a spirited charge led by Custer, which silenced the battery, drove off the defending Confederates, and resulted in the mortal wounding of Stuart. In September Custer's brigade helped spearhead Sheridan's advance up the Shenandoah Valley against forces under Jubal Early. On 30 September, after the capture of Winchester, Custer was given command of the Third Cavalry Division.[14]

In the spring of 1865, Custer's division was among those most active in bringing to bay Robert E. Lee and the tired and depleted Army of Northern Virginia. On 7 April, acting on information acquired from a captured Confederate straggler—and in defiance of orders from his immediate superior, Wesley Merritt[15]—Custer rushed his division forward, throwing it between Lee and his only line of retreat through Appomattox Court House. Lee surrendered on 9 April. Sheridan showed his appreciation of Custer's efforts by purchasing from Wilmer McLean, the owner of the house in which Lee surrendered to Grant, the table on which the surrender terms had been written and signed, and presenting it as a gift to Libbie. Custer bore the table off on his shoulder, carrying in his pocket a note from Sheridan to Libbie:

> I respectfully present to you the small writing table on which the conditions for surrender of the Confederate Army of Northern Virginia were written by Lt. General Grant—and permit me to say, Madam, that there is scarcely an individual in our service who has contributed more to bring about this desirable result than your very gallant husband.[16]

Thus, for the Custers, the war ended. During its four years, George Armstrong Custer had experienced a meteoric rise from being an unknown second lieutenant of little obvious promise to a brevet major general and major general of volunteers. His name, if not quite a household word, was at least very well known in the eastern and middlewestern states. He owed much of his success to his courage and daring and immense energy, but he also developed real skills. These were largely tactical skills: he was unusually capable of reading the terrain, and he was a military opportunist, quick to grasp an opening when it was offered. The seemingly persistent element of luck contributed to the pattern: the phrase "Custer's luck" became almost proverbial. Too much has perhaps been made of this, however. It was certainly fortunate for Custer that he came into relatively close contact with able and experienced superiors as a very young officer, yet little would have come of these relationships if he had not had military talent and skills. Victories in actual combat situations usually derived from Custer's ability.

One point of some characterological interest is worth special note. Custer occasionally acted in a way which brushed aside or exceeded the limits of what his immediate superiors had ordered or expected. When it came to the event, however, Custer usually carried it off; his actions often were successful, and thus he usually looked good in the eyes of his superiors' superiors—McClellan, Pleasonton, and Sheridan. To a high-ranking officer who appeared to know his job, Custer would give unquestioning loyalty.

EIGHT

The Plains Years

IN the immediate postwar months Custer, retaining his temporary rank and serving under Sheridan, was engaged in garrison duty and reconstruction activities in Louisiana and Texas. These activities offered little scope for his talents or energy, but they permitted Custer and Libbie to enjoy a quieter life than they had hitherto known. Then, in January 1866, Custer's volunteer commission expired, and he was reduced in rank and pay to a captain in the Regular Army.[1] This was a distressing development; during May, Custer, who had obtained a thirty-day leave of absence, sought in various ways to better himself. He sensibly declined several business offers, realizing that his temperament and abilities were unsuited to such employment. He thought that he had found what he was seeking when he learned that the revolutionary army of Benito Juarez was looking for a chief of cavalry and was willing to pay $16,000 a year in gold. Custer probably could have obtained the position, having been given a fine letter of recommendation by General Grant, but he could not follow through on his application. The United States army, having a plethora of officers, would not give him indefinite leave, and abandoning the economic security it afforded did not seem attractive to him.[2]

Having fallen to minimum strength by early 1866, the army was then expanded slightly through the establishment of several new cavalry regiments. Custer applied for the new position of inspector general of cavalry. His application was turned down. This was a difficult time for Custer. After the disappointments of not being given a permanent commission as a general officer and of being denied the leave which would have permitted him to accept the Mexican offer came this third rebuff. The truth was that Custer's talents lay in combat leadership, and what the army needed now in its general officers was administrative ability. Other temporary generals such as Terry, with war records in no way superior to Custer's, nevertheless had better reputations for levelheadedness and organizational capacity. Custer had not done particularly well in his postwar assignment, and this fact presumably counted against him. On 28 July 1866, however, Custer received a promotion to the permanent rank of lieutenant colonel.[3] Given a choice of regiments, he elected to serve with the newly authorized Seventh Cavalry. This was far from the status he had hoped for, but it was the best option available.

During the latter part of 1866 Custer dabbled briefly in politics. He aligned himself with the National Union party of President Andrew Johnson, and in fact was a delegate from Michigan to its convention in Philadelphia. Later he accepted Johnson's invitation to accompany the presidential party on a railroad tour of the country. Grant was among the several officers who appeared with the president, but, whether because of trouble with his drinking or because feelers were already being extended to him with respect to a political future, he left the train before the end of the tour. This brief political exposure did Custer more harm than good, for Johnson was in no position to help him, and the Republicans were alienated.[4]

When Custer joined the Seventh Cavalry toward the end of 1866, the regiment was still being organized; it had been authorized specifically for the purpose of fighting Indians. The colonel of the regiment was Andrew J. Smith, a veteran in his fifties. The regimental headquarters were at Fort Riley, Kansas, on the Kaw (Kansas) River. Fort Riley was in the Department of the Missouri, commanded by Brig. Gen. W. S. Hancock, with headquarters at Fort Leavenworth; the department was one of the four military areas comprising the Division of Missouri, whose commanding general at this time was William T. Sherman. As noted earlier, Custer had difficulties from the first with some of his principal subordinate officers. For one thing, many of these men were older than Custer and, like him, were smarting under the indignity of demotion from more important commands during the Civil War. Custer's flamboyant and sometimes abrasive personality also caused problems. It was not that he did not make a conscious attempt to get along with his subordinates; he did. In fact, Libbie records a number of occasions on which her husband was mindful of the value of good relations with them, and he often deliberately refrained from informing her of professional or personal difficulties lest she, in her partisanship, snub offending officers or their wives. The fact remains, however, that Custer himself seems not to have had the knack of working smoothly with officers junior in rank but senior in age.

Captains Benteen and Robert M. West were among the anti-Custer officers from the very beginning. Like Benteen, West was older than Custer and had been a brevet brigadier general during the Civil War. He did not take his demotion well, was status conscious, and drank more than was good for him. Another officer who disliked Custer was the senior major, Wyckliffe Cooper. This lanky Kentuckian had also held higher commands during the war, and, like West, was an alcoholic.[5] Custer, once he had become a teetotaler, was intolerant of drinking among his officers and men. There was always a strong pro-Custer faction in the regiment as well. Officers in this group included Captains Tom Custer, George Yates, Myles Keogh, and Myles Moylan.[6] The junior major, Joel Elliott, was neither pro-Custer nor anti-Custer, merely a good officer doing his duty. This young man had enlisted as a private in the Civil War. He rose to be a captain and he had recently passed a qualifying examination for all regular officers with such a brilliant score than he was made a major.[7] (Custer, of course, had taken the same examination.) Thus Elliott was in the position, peculiar for this period, of receiving a higher rank in the postwar army than he had held during the war.

In the spring of 1867, in response to intense pressure from the citizens of Kansas and other frontier states and territories, the War Department authorized Sherman to send military expeditions to subdue and intimidate those Indians showing armed resistance to the advancing white settlers. As a principal part of this effort, General Hancock mounted a large expedition of infantry, cavalry, and artillery. To understand Custer's activities and motives in this campaign, it is necessary to have in mind a picture of the geography involved. The area of the Seventh Cavalry's campaign on this occasion was vast, involving northern Kansas, southern Nebraska, and the northeastern portion of the Territory of Colorado. The country is chiefly prairie, rising from east to west at an average of eight or nine feet per mile, and is dominated by two river systems. These are the Kansas River, with its two principal tributaries, the Smoky Hill River (virtually an extension of the Kansas) to the south and the Republican River to the north, and the Platte River, with its southern fork, the South Platte. The Kansas-Smokey Hill river system runs a fairly straight course across the middle of Kansas and into Colorado for a total of more than 500 miles. Roughly 150 miles to the north runs the Platte-South Platte system. Almost midway between these two arteries, but closer to the Platte, runs the Republican for most of its western course. Along both the Platte-South Platte system and the Kansas-Smoky Hill system was a series of forts. From east to west along the Platte were Forts Kearny, McPherson, and Sedgwick; along the Kansas-Smoky Hill axis were Forts Riley, Harker, Hays, and Wallace. The Republican River country was wilder and less settled and had no fortified posts. Fort Leavenworth, General Hancock's headquarters, still stands on the Missouri River, a short distance above the mouth of the Kansas.

Hancock's expedition left Fort Leavenworth on 1 March 1867. At Fort Riley it picked up the Seventh Cavalry with Smith and Custer. Field headquarters were established at Fort Larned, Kansas, on the Arkansas River about 60 miles south of Fort Hays and about 250 miles west of Fort Leavenworth. Here Colonel Smith was retained for detached service, and Custer and the Seventh Cavalry were sent out to the northwest to find and defeat the hostile Indians. Custer scouted north to Fort Hays, waiting there for supplies—and also for Libbie, to whom he had sent word of his route. After nearly a month Custer continued north in search of the Indians, taking seven companies (troops) with him. He found no hostiles, and he established camp on the Platte near Fort McPherson. On 16 June, General Sherman arrived for a visit. He ordered Custer to search the watershed of the Republican River, a favorite Indian hunting ground.[8]

Custer set off on the scout with orders to report for his next instructions to Fort Sedgwick, on the Platte at the Nebraska-Colorado border, about 100 miles due west of Fort McPherson. The intended scout would form roughly three sides of a rectangle, with one leg overland to the Republican River, one leg along that stream westward, and one leg northward to Fort Sedgwick. Custer looked eagerly for the hostile Indians, but they were not to be found. He made camp on the upper Republican and took stock of his situation. He needed supplies; he was anxious to see Libbie. He decided to send supply wagons under guard south to Fort Wallace,

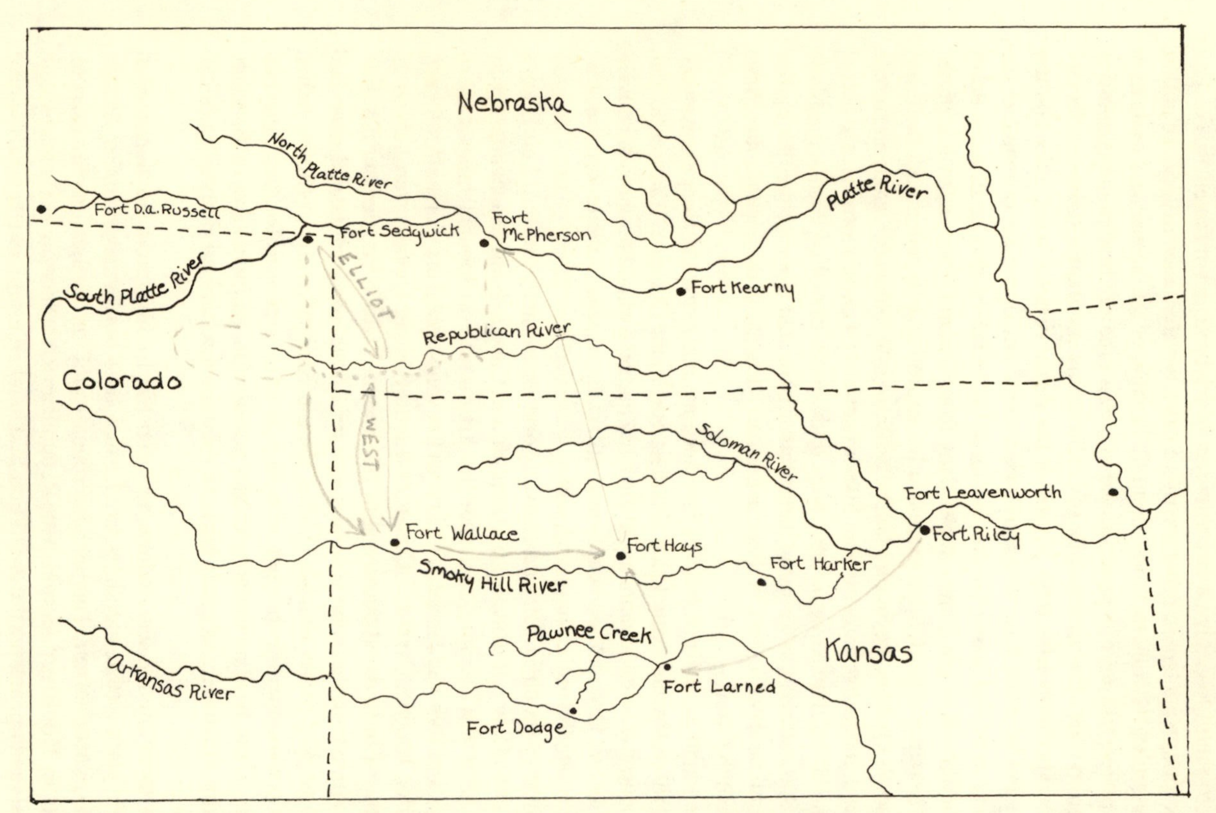

Area of the Seventh Cavalry's Campaign against the Plains Indians. After Lawrence A.. Frost, *The Court-Martial of General George Armstrong Custer*. *By permission of the author and the University of Oklahoma Press. Copyright 1968 by the University of Oklahoma Press, Publishing Division of the University.*

instead of going north to Fort Sedgwick as ordered. Troopers under Captain West formed the escort, but Custer placed the whole unit—wagon train plus troopers—under the command of his adjutant, Lt. W. W. Cooke. West, the ranking officer, thus had to report to Cooke, a circumstance which he deeply resented.[9]

The wagon escort was to bring word to Libbie, who had been asked to be at Fort Hays, to return with them to his camp.[10] In view of the hostile and unscouted territory she would have to traverse, and in view of the fact that the campaign was by no means over, this summoning of Libbie was a remarkable decision. Shortly after the expedition left camp, Custer learned that hostiles were indeed in the vicinity, and he must have wondered what might be happening to Libbie if she were doing as he had asked. Custer also sent Major Elliott with a small escort north to Fort Sedgwick to get further instructions from General Sherman by telegraph. Elliott performed his mission successfully, returning with orders that the command was to continue farther up the Republican into Colorado, scouting for the Indians and giving battle if possible. Soon afterward the supply wagons and escort returned, having had to fight their way back north from Fort Wallace against several war parties. Cooke told Custer that Libbie had not received his earlier message to come out to Fort Wallace and in fact had gone in the opposite direction, back to Fort Riley.[11]

Custer set off as ordered, but at a feverish pace. He pushed his men excessively and then unwisely made camp near a road leading to the Colorado gold mines. The troopers began deserting at once. On the early morning of 7 July, about thirty men deserted before reveille had been sounded. At noon, after a fifteen-mile march, another group left for the stage road, some of them on their horses. Custer shouted to the officer of the day, "Stop those men! Shoot them where you find them. Don't bring in any alive." Elliott, Tom Custer, Cooke, and a few troopers rode off in pursuit. After a while they returned, bringing in five prisoners, three of them wounded. Ten men had escaped. The prisoners were loaded onto a wagon. "Don't go near that wagon, Doctor," Custer said loudly as the command was about to move out. "I have no sympathy with those men." Later the surgeon did give professional assistance to the injured troopers without hindrance from Custer, but one of them died of his wounds.[12] That night Custer ordered his officers, rather than as was usual the enlisted men, to walk post and to shoot anyone who came out of his tent. There were no further attempts at desertion, partly because of the harsh disciplinary measures and partly because the command was now farther from the stage road.

Still without finding any Indians to fight, but having found the bodies of a messenger party commanded by Lt. Lyman S. Kidder (the so-called Kidder Massacre), Custer turned south and made his way to Fort Wallace, the last outpost on the Smoky Hill River. Here he learned that cholera had broken out at Fort Riley and was spreading through the area. Instead of sending Libbie instructions to go as far east as necessary to get entirely out of danger, Custer decided to go see her himself.[13] There were problems at Fort Wallace. The horses of the command were tired, and some of them were near exhaustion from the long forced marches. The supply of food was low, which was believed would make the men more susceptible to cholera.[14] These circumstances provided Custer with a rationalization for leaving his command without orders to do so. There can be little question, however, that his major motive was to see Libbie, for it would have been perfectly feasible to have again sent out a supply expedition while remaining with his command in the field.

Custer started on the 150-mile trip to Fort Hays, with the wagon train and an escort, at sunset on 15 July. They marched all night and all of the next day and night with only brief halts. Then Custer of necessity slowed the pace slightly; however, they covered the entire distance in sixty hours, with but six hours' rest. At Downer's Station, about 35 miles west of Fort Hays, a few stragglers from the column were cut off by Indians. Custer did not turn back for them when this was reported, but asked an infantry patrol at the station to do so.[15]

Supplies were inadequate at Fort Hays. Custer then told Capt. Louis Hamilton to continue to Fort Harker with the wagons and escort. He himself, with Tom Custer, Cooke, and two troopers, set out for Harker at a much faster pace. They reached the fort the next morning at 2:00. There was a railhead at Fort Harker, and the train east to Fort Riley left in an hour. Custer went immediately to Colonel Smith's quarters, roused him and told him the wagon train was coming, and asked his permission to go on to Fort Riley, saying that he would be back to organize the loading of the wagons. Perhaps not being fully awake, the old colonel granted permission, something which he had no authority to do nor Custer any right to ask. Later that morning, after thinking it over, Smith wired Custer to return at once. Having had his visit with Libbie, Custer did so. Shortly afterward, on 28 July, he was arrested by order of General Hancock for his unauthorized moves.[16]

At Hancock's instructions, Smith preferred charges against Custer and a court-martial was arranged. Hancock's military efforts that summer had not been a success, which provoked some public clamor, and Lawrence Frost has hypothesized that Custer was to be sacrificed to quiet this dissatisfaction. Some such motive may have influenced Hancock, but it seems unlikely that it was his sole motive. There was little connection between Custer's disobedience—or other aspects of his conduct, whatever one may think of them—and the unsatisfactory outcome of the expedition. The whole situation was complicated by Captain West, who was still smarting from the Cooke incident and who had been reprimanded several times by Custer for his drinking habits. West preferred additional charges on his own initiative.[17]

The court-martial was convened at Fort Leavenworth, Kansas, on 15 September 1867. The senior officer was Bvt. Maj. Gen. William Hoffman, colonel, Third U.S. Infantry. Among the ten officers detailed to serve on the court were also two high-ranking cavalrymen, Cols. John W. Davidson and Benjamin H. Grierson. Custer was charged by Hancock with "absence without leave from his command" and "conduct to the prejudice of good order and military discipline." In addition (as was technically correct, though somewhat unusual), he was charged by

Captain West with "conduct prejudicial to good order and military discipline." In brief, Hancock's charges referred to Custer's absenting himself from his command on personal business, but West's were more serious, referring among other items to Custer's having ordered "enlisted men of his command to be shot down as supposed deserters . . . without trial" and causing "three men to be severely wounded." West also specified that "Custer did order and cause" three troopers "to be placed in a government wagon, and to be hauled eighteen miles (and did then and there neglect and positively and persistently refuse to allow the said soldiers to receive treatment and attention from the Acting Assistant Surgeon with his command or any other Medical or Surgical attendance whatever)."[18]

Custer pleaded not guilty to all of the charges and specifications—a curious circumstance, since many of them were factually correct. Without attempting to be legalistic about it, one would have supposed that a plea of "guilty, but with significant mitigating circumstances" would have been more appropriate. A favorable deposition by Major Elliott was introduced by the accused.[19] Much testimony was heard and the customary addresses to the court were made by counsels for the defense and for the prosecution. Custer and his counsel did not attempt to refute any of the actions with which he had been charged, but they did attempt to justify them.

Final arguments were heard on 11 October, and, after a relatively brief deliberation, the court found Custer guilty of all charges and specifications except the specification of Custer's not permitting medical assistance to the wounded men. The verdict was sent to higher authority for review, and on 18 November Lieutenant General Sherman offered a formal comment: "The proceedings, findings, and sentence in the case of Brevet Major General Custer are approved by General Grant . . . the levity of the sentence, considering the nature of the offenses of Bvt. Major General Custer if found guilty is to be remarked on."[20]

The verdict, like the court-martial itself, seems not to have been consciously expected by Custer. It was a hard blow, not only materially—for he had little money—but more especially to his pride. (Stewart has referred to Custer as having received "a deep spiritual wound" on this occasion.)[21] Sheridan, who had been posted to Fort Leavenworth to succeed Hancock, gave the Custers the use of his fine new quarters, and this generous action helped ease their financial situation. Sheridan expressed an intention also to do something about the humiliating verdict, writing to Custer from Ohio: "I will be in Washington the 20th of this month. I hope to be able to look into your case a little more—even against your will—I had no reason to suppose any such punishment would be awarded when I wrote from New York."[22] Sheridan, however, was astute in military politics, and one gets the impression that he considered it not in his own best interests either to have made it his business to learn more about the case earlier or to press hard later for any amelioration of the sentence.

The Custers stayed at Fort Leavenworth during the winter and spring, attempting to make the best of things. They did some entertaining and were entertained in turn. In June they went to Monroe and remained there during the summer. Then, with autumn, there came a welcome telegram from Sheridan. Writing from Fort Hays, Kansas, on 24 September 1868, he told Custer:

> Generals Sherman, Sully, and myself, and nearly all the officers of your regiment, have asked for you, and I hope the applications will be successful. Can you come at once? Eleven companies of your regiment will move about the first of October against the hostile Indians, from Medicine Lodge Creek toward the Washita mountain.[23]

Custer left for Fort Hays the next morning. Sheridan's request was approved; the official order overtook Custer on the train, and he reported for duty on 30 September. Several days later he wrote to Libbie: "I breakfasted with Genl. Sheridan and staff. He said, 'Custer, I rely on leaving you to act entirely on your own judgement.'"[24]

The Seventh Cavalry, Custer learned, was at Fort Dodge on the Arkansas River, some 90 miles to the southwest of Fort Hays. Sheridan planned to establish an outpost 100 miles still farther south in the Indian territory. When cold weather set in, hampering the Indians' mobility, Custer was to go out after them.[25] As always, there was tension in the regiment. Captain West, somewhat surprisingly in view of the circumstances, was still there, and so was Captain Benteen. But so were Tom Custer and Yates, Weir, Keogh, Moylan, and Cooke, while Major Elliott could always be counted on to do his duty as a loyal officer.

The expedition left to establish Camp Supply on 12 November 1868, Brigadier General Sully commanding.[26] It moved south and a little west for the better part of six days. On 18 November it halted where Wolf and Beaver creeks unite to form the North Fork of the Canadian River. Here plans were drawn up for a fort. On 23 November, Custer set out, still moving south toward the Washita River. He took with him eleven companies of the Seventh Cavalry, numbering about 800 officers and men. He also took some Osage scouts and a small train of wagons. On the evening of the twenty-fourth the command camped on the Canadian River (or South Fork of the Canadian River, as it also was called). Early on the twenty-fifth, Custer sent Major Elliott and three companies on a scout along the river banks while he supervised the crossing of the river by the wagon train. Around noon, one of Elliott's scouts rode up with the news that a fresh trail had been found. It was estimated that it represented 150 warriors.[27] They were riding south, probably headed for a village on the Washita.

Custer ordered Elliott to follow the trail until 8:00 P.M. and then wait until the main body of the command caught up. As it turned out, it was 9:00 P.M. when the whole command was reunited at a point on the Washita. It had snowed just before the command left Fort Supply; it was cold at the river, and the snow was crusted. At 10:00 P.M. Custer moved his forces out to follow the trail by moonlight. Because of the crunching of the horses' hooves in the crusted snow, Custer had the scouts move well ahead of the column. After five miles or so, the scouts spied the still burning coals of a campfire. The command halted, and Custer and two of the scouts advanced a bit further. In the quiet night they heard a dog barking and then a baby crying. The village lay just ahead.[28]

It was now a little past midnight. Custer divided the command into four battalions. Elliott, taking one battalion, was to approach the village from the far side. Another unit was to approach from the right side and a third from the left. Custer would lead the fourth battalion directly forward. The attack took place at dawn and seems to have achieved complete surprise. The troopers rode into the village from four sides and fired at the warriors as they rushed from their tents. Some of the Indians rallied quickly, and, taking cover behind trees or in sinkholes, began returning the fire. The fight lasted for two or three hours as a general engagement, and then it was over except for sporadic firing.[29]

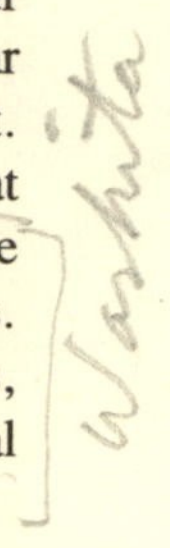

The village proved to be that of Black Kettle of the Southern Cheyenne. Indian casualties were heavy, especially among the warriors, of whom there seem to have been several hundred, but a number of women and children were also killed or wounded. However, the horrors were not all one-sided. One Indian woman, attempting to escape with a small white boy (a prisoner), produced a long knife and disemboweled the boy on the spot when she was thwarted in her flight. On searching the tepees, the troopers found many relics of Kansas homesteads which had been attacked by the Indians.[30]

By noon it was becoming apparent that Black Kettle's was not a solitary village, but one of a group strung out along the Washita valley, for additional warriors were beginning to appear on the hills nearby. How large this force might become was entirely unknown to Custer's command. Custer had the captured Indian women and children select horses from the village herd, and then had the troopers destroy the remaining Indian horses and tear down and burn the tepees and such stores as they contained. Toward dusk he assembled the regiment at the center of the village site. It was then discovered that Major Elliott and about sixteen troopers were missing. Several officers recalled having seen Elliott and the men riding off earlier in the day in pursuit of some fleeing warriors.[31]

The number of Indians on the hills had increased considerably. The wagon train, almost unguarded, was miles away. No firing could be heard at this time. A victory had been won, but possible defeat loomed ahead. Exactly what passed through Custer's mind cannot be certainly known, but his major concern was to extricate his command from the dangerous situation in which it now found itself. The search for Elliott and his little band was limited to the village and the ground immediately outside it. (Pro-Custer officers later said that the search extended to a two-mile perimeter.) Custer then ordered that a show be made of advancing toward the nearest Indian village. With the band playing, the command started to move forward. The Indians retreated along the bluffs. As soon as the darkness became complete, Custer had the regiment countermarch, retracing the steps by which they had first come to the village. The ruse succeeded; the command was not pursued. By 2:00 A.M. it was far enough from the village to halt briefly and build fires, and by 10:00 A.M. it had rejoined the wagon train. There they made camp.[32]

On 1 December the command returned to Camp Supply. Sheridan rode out to meet them and congratulate Custer. Sherman wired congratulations.[33] The reputations of Custer and of the Seventh Cavalry as Indian fighters were established. Nonetheless, public opinion of their actions and the policy they represented differed greatly. Should the fight at the Washita be considered a meritorious achievement, markedly reducing the likelihood of Indian depredations in the southern plains, or was it a barbarous and unnecessary way of producing safety along the southern frontier? Answers divided along geographic lines and according to whether individuals supported the army or the Indian Bureau. In general, those in the Midwest and West backed the military solution, whereas there was strong criticism of it in much of the East.

Custer seems to have been only moderately affected by these stormy differences of opinion. His superiors generally approved of what he had done, and so did most of the people among whom he passed his life. There was, however, a specific negative criticism which touched him deeply. There were those who said that Custer should have noticed Major Elliott's absence sooner, and there were others who said that, even if he had not been apprised of the missing unit until late in the day, he should have made a more sustained effort to find it. Captain Benteen wrote an unsigned letter, published in the *Saint Louis Missouri Democrat* on 9 February 1869, which took Custer severely to task for not having tried to save Elliott and his troopers.[34] When Custer eventually saw it, he was visibly shaken. He summoned his officers, said that he was certain that one of them must have written the letter, and threatened to horsewhip the one who had done so. Benteen said that he had written the article—an interesting admission—and Custer, after staring at him for a moment, surprisingly left the room.[35]

Thus, psychologically speaking, the Washita expedition had two aspects for Custer. The first was that it greatly enhanced his fame and that of his regiment. The second, slower to develop, was that it produced some adverse public criticism and heightened tensions within the regiment.

The period between 1869 and 1874 was, for Custer, one of partial eclipse, with numerous dissatisfactions, some major and some minor. A major dissatisfaction was his failure to receive a promotion. In this matter Custer had plenty of company; yet, for one who was used to moving up the ladder faster than anyone else, the situation must have been especially galling. Moreover, some others were still advancing. Young Elliott, for example, had moved to his highest rank after the Civil War. By early 1869 Sherman had been made a full general and chief of staff; Sheridan had been made a lieutenant general—and Grant had been elected president. Custer kept trying, but his efforts were unsuccessful. In 1869, for instance, he applied for the position of commandant of West Point, but the application was refused. His boredom and dissatisfaction were evinced during this period by his repeatedly requesting long leaves of absence. The years 1871 and 1872 were particularly stultifying. There was plenty of social and recreational activity, but professionally it was a dreary time. Custer was stationed in Elizabethtown, Kentucky, with only two companies of the Seventh Cavalry, and given the task of suppressing the local Ku Klux Klan.[36] Partly to offset his boredom, he began writing articles for *Galaxy* magazine, some of which showed considerable, albeit conventional, literary ability. They later formed the basis for his book, *My Life on the Plains*.

In 1873 there was a period of action starting with Custer's transfer to the Department of Dakota, in which he would serve for the brief remainder of his life. The Northern Pacific Railroad was in the building, and the next phase called for its extension across Sioux territory, following the Yellowstone River. The army was called upon to protect the surveyors, and the Seventh Cavalry was reunited at Memphis, then proceeding to Fort Rice, Dakota Territory. Commanded by Col. (Bvt. Maj. Gen.) David S. Stanley, the expedition consisted of twenty companies of infantry, ten of cavalry (under Custer), Indian scouts, the Northern Pacific engineers, a large wagon train, and a herd of beef cattle.[37]

The expedition started from Fort Rice on 20 June 1873, headed for the north bank of the Yellowstone River. There was trouble between Stanley and Custer almost from the first. Custer disliked Stanley's drinking and Stanley found Custer insufferable. The situation was intensified by the fact that it was the cavalry's natural and assigned task to do the scouting and pathfinding, occupations in which Custer excelled. This meant that at least a portion of the cavalry regularly would be riding ahead of the rest of the command. Custer took advantage of the situation, at times acting almost as if he had an independent command. At one point, being about fifteen miles in advance of the infantry, Custer in effect sent Stanley orders for forage and rations to be sent up to him. Stanley reacted by placing Custer under temporary arrest.[38] When his freedom was restored, Custer again used the naturally greater mobility of the cavalry to get into semi-independent actions—successful ones—against several bands of hostile Sioux. Later he persuaded Stanley to let him strike out across country on a separate mission with six companies of cavalry. As in some earlier situations, Custer's energy and effectiveness made it difficult for a slower-moving—and perhaps slower-thinking—immediate superior to hold him in rein.

The next swing upward in Custer's fortunes came in the summer of 1874. Rumors of gold in the Black Hills (reserved to the Sioux Nation in the treaty of 1868) and protestations from frontier settlers, particularly in Nebraska, over Indian raids led the administration to authorize an expedition. Its stated purpose was to scout the Black Hills country with an eye to establishing a military outpost, "so that," in the words of Sheridan, "by holding an interior point in the heart of the Indian country we could threaten the villages and stock of the Indians, if they made raids on our settlements in Nebraska." Unofficially the expedition was to investigate the possibility of gold deposits. Under instructions from Generals Sheridan and Terry, the expedition, under Custer's command, set out from Fort Abraham Lincoln, Dakota Territory, on 2 July 1874. The command consisted of ten troops of the Seventh Cavalry, two companies of infantry, three Gatling guns and a three-inch field piece with their crews, Indian scouts, and a large wagon train and herd of cattle. There also were specialized personnel: engineers under Captain Ludlow, the man to whom Custer was later to confide his impulse to "swing clear" of General Terry, geologists, zoologists, and two miners.[39]

The expedition encountered no hostile Indians. It marched in a large figure eight, moving from Fort Lincoln southwest across what is now North Dakota to a point just across the border of Montana Territory, then straight south for a couple of hundred miles into Wyoming Territory. It then moved east, across the Wyoming boundary into the Black Hills. After exploring this region the command went almost due north, crossing its outward-bound track and eventually striking the Heart River, and then moving east, back to Fort Lincoln. The command reached headquarters on 30 August, having traveled a distance of 883 miles in fifty-nine days. Counting side trips made without the wagon train, the total number of miles surveyed came to 1,205.[40]

The high point of the expedition, historically speaking, occurred 30 July, when gold was discovered. At first the traces were faint, but by 3 August an area was found in which the miners estimated that a prospecter might be able to pan gold at the rate of seventy-five dollars a day (perhaps twelve times that in today's values).[41] Custer drafted a report to Sheridan, stating in part:

> As there are scientists accompanying the expedition who are examining into the mineral resources of this region . . . I omit all present reference to that portion of our explorations . . . except to state . . . that gold has been found in many places, and it is the belief of those who are giving their attention to this subject that it will be found in paying quantities. . . . Veins of lead and strong indications of the existence of silver have been found. Until further examination is made regarding the richness of the gold, no opinion should be formed.[42]

Charlie Reynolds, a scout who had been sent with the expedition for the purpose, rode off with this dispatch. Riding by night, in ninety-six hours he reached Fort Laramie, whence the message was telegraphed to Sheridan. On 13 August Reynolds arrived at Sioux City, Iowa, and there he gave interviews to newspapermen. By evening his reports were on the front pages of several newspapers. The *Yankton Press and Dakotian* printed enthusiastic headlines.

STRUCK IT AT LAST!
Rich Mines of Gold and Silver
Reported Found by Custer

PREPARE FOR LIVELY TIMES!
Gold Expected to Fall 10 per cent.—
Spades and Picks Rising.—The
National Debt to be Paid
When Custer Returns.[43]

The whole country had been watching the expedition; westerners in particular were eager for news of a gold strike, primarily because of the business opportunities likely to come in its wake. The government (and so the army) had maintained that the expedition was to reconnoiter, which was permitted under the treaty. But the spirit of the expedition violated the agreement, since the establishment of a military post deep in Sioux territory and the influx of prospectors, whether officially sanctioned or not, was not envisioned by it. All the expedition had really accomplished was to give the army a virtually impossible task: to keep the prospectors out of the Black Hills area while confining the Indians to it. Custer's reputation was undeniably enhanced by the mission, again particularly in the Midwest and West, although he also had a staunch booster in James Gordon Bennett of the Democratic *New York Herald*.

These were tense times politically. The Democrats had control of Congress, the Republicans of the White House. The scandals of Grant's administration were beginning to become noticeable, and the attempt to make political capital of them was about to begin. It was in this setting that the effort to impeach Secretary of War Belknap took shape.

NINE

Marriage and Domestic Life

It is fair to say that no thorough understanding of George Armstrong Custer is possible without a close consideration of his marriage to Elizabeth Bacon. It is fortunate for the historian that both husband and wife wrote voluminously and often revealingly. Much of this material remains in the collections of the Custer family and of Lawrence A. Frost, a long-time friend of the family. Much personal material, however, is available in several books. Custer's own memoir, *My Life on the Plains,* is only indirectly helpful, since it concentrates on his professional activities. On the other hand, Elizabeth B. Custer's *''Boots and Saddles'', Tenting on the Plains,* and *Following the Guidon* are extremely pertinent, containing many firsthand anecdotes and quoting correspondence. Two other authors, having had access to many of Custer's and Elizabeth's letters, quote from these sources directly and extensively: Marguerite Merington in *The Custer Story* and Lawrence A. Frost in *General Custer's Libbie*.

By all accounts, Elizabeth (''Libbie'') Bacon was a very bright and a very pretty girl, gently reared, the only daughter of a relatively old and decidedly prominent father. She was somewhat spoiled, and at the same time, having lost her mother and being without brothers or sisters, she was also emotionally deprived. She was no doubt used to getting what she wanted in most things—and she wanted Custer. It was she who first spoke to him, and later it was she who had the courage to become privately engaged to him against her father's wishes.

Libbie considered herself something of a tomboy. She spoke disparagingly (how sincerely one does not know) of her body, complaining that she did not have the generous curves so much admired in her day. At times she was able to express humorous satisfaction with her leanness, as when she described what happened when she and a girlfriend, taking a stroll at dusk outside a frontier fort, were mistaken by sentries for Indians and fired upon. At the first shots the young women threw themselves upon the ground. ''The pretty, rounded contour of the girl, which she had naturally taken such delight in, was now a source of agony to her, and she moaned out, 'Oh! how high I seem to be above you! Oh, Libbie, do you think I lie as flat to the ground as you do?''[1]

Libbie apparently felt confined, perhaps not very useful or needed in her home environment, and she longed for an adventurous life. When she fell in love, there evidently was a strong identification with her loved one. This is suggested by her tendency to become immediately involved in Custer's difficulties with his junior officers. At the first hint of anyone's being antagonistic to her husband, that person was immediately Libbie's enemy. Custer was certainly not the soul of tact, and yet Libbie mentions instances in which he clearly felt it necessary to caution her not to show such displeasure in social settings. Thus she wrote to Custer on 5 April 1867: ''You will laugh at my religion, I'm afraid, when I tell you that I hurried out of church, so as not to be obliged to speak to your enemy! But do not be worried; I will do what you wish; I will go and call on his wife, and do the polite.''[2]

Libbie also idealized her husband. The identification and the idealization emerge clearly from her writings and from her life, during both her marriage and her fifty-seven-year widowhood. Her books are filled with her husband. They contain high praise, sometimes extravagantly high, and not a word of intentional criticism. Libbie was totally involved in her husband's life: his family was her family; his regiment, her regiment. Tom Custer is always ''our brother,'' Maggie Custer Calhoun always ''our sister,'' and when Libbie wrote, ''Two of our number brought their wives back to camp,'' the two with whom she identifies are, of course, fellow officers of Custer.[3] After Custer's death, Libbie was preoccupied with defending his reputation and making sure his name endured. She was gratified when the decision was made to remove Custer's remains to West Point and erect a large statue in his memory. (Although she was displeased at the actual statue, considering it unflattering.)[4] She was further pleased when she was informed that she could be buried beside her husband, and she insisted that her own grave be given only a small and simple marker. She attended with pleasure when an equestrian statue of Custer was placed in the town square of Monroe, but she never returned after the statue was moved to a less prominent position some years later.

Libbie was aware of the process of identification from early in the marriage. She was a little afraid of it and tried to rationalize. In October 1864, she wrote:

> Remember, I cannot love you as I do without my life blending into yours. I would not lose my individuality, but would be, as a wife should be, part of her husband, a life within a life. I was never an admirer of a submissive wife, but I wish to look to my husband as superior in judgment and experience and to be guided by him in all things.[5]

Libbie was outgoing and quite unashamed of her physical attraction to her husband. The principal description she gave of Custer in ''*Boots and Saddles*'' is intensely physical.

> He was at this time [1874] thirty-five years of age, weighed 170 pounds, and was nearly six feet in height. His eyes were clear blue and deeply set; his hair, short, wavy, and golden

in tint. His mustache was long and tawny in color; his complexion was florid, except where his forehead was shaded by his hat, for the sun always burned his skin ruthlessly.

He was the most agile, active man I ever knew, and so very strong and in such perfect physical condition that he rarely knew even an hour's indisposition.

Horse and man seemed one when the general vaulted into the saddle. His body was so lightly poised and so full of swinging, undulating motion, it almost seemed that the wind moved him as it blew over the plain. Yet every nerve was alert and like finely tempered steel, for the muscles and sinews that seemed so pliable were equal to the curbing of the most fiery animal.[6]

Soon after they were married, Libbie wrote from Washington to Custer in the field in June 1864.

My darling Boy. . . . I suppose that some rebel is devouring my epistles, but I am too grateful to feel badly about that. Let me unburden my mind about the matter, since your last letter implies chiding, tho the slightest and kindliest. No Southerner could say, if they are *gentlemen* that I lacked refinement. There can be nothing low between man and wife if they love each other. What I wrote was holy and sacred. Only cruel people would not understand the spirit in which I wrote it.[7]

The issue did not immediately recede, for Libbie recurs to it in July.

I shall not again offend my dear boy's sense of nicety by departing from that delicate propriety which, I believe, was born in me—the lady in me inherited from my mother. . . . Trust me, my dear. I am glad you are particular with me. With my much loved and honored parents I felt indignant at reproof, but when you express yourself as ever so slightly displeased I feel grieved and try to do better.[8]

Fascinating sentences, these, in which the highly bred and beautiful young bride reacts to finding that her hardy cavalryman husband has been offended by her passionate letters. One can only assume that whatever gratification Custer may have experienced at receiving these messages was not sufficient to outweigh his anxiety lest he be made fun of if they were intercepted.

There can be no doubt that Custer loved Libbie; in fact, she was indispensable to him. The quality of the love is, however, a matter of interest. There seems to have been, on his part, a good bit of romanticizing, idealizing, and pampering. Libbie spent much on her wardrobe, for example, and although she had a little money of her own, most of this expense was borne by her husband. Custer wanted very much to think of Libbie as a lady, and he was opposed to her doing domestic work. Libbie observed: "Domestic care sat very lightly with me. Nothing seemed to annoy my husband more than to find me in the kitchen. He determinedly opposed it for years and begged me to make a promise that I would never go there for more than a moment."[9]

Custer's letters to Libbie are also revealing. In general they are well-written, affectionate, newsy letters with many anecdotes. Usually they are decorous, but they sometimes included an erotic note. For example, in a letter written in the spring of 1867, Custer mentioned various things which he hoped Libbie would bring to an expected rendezvous, such as a croquet set, butter, and fresh vegetables, and then went on: "I know *something* much, very much better and be sure you bring *it* along. *I am entirely out at present,* and have been for so long as to almost forget how it tastes. . . . Remember, every moment gone can never be reclaimed."[10]

Perhaps the most striking feature of Custer's letters is their frequent, only thinly veiled bragging.

The other day at the close of my successful fight near Front Royal I was riding with staff and escort near Ramson's battery, now with my brigade, and which was in a fight with me for the first time. . . . They are all regulars, who, you may not be aware, are stoical and undemonstrative. But imagine my surprise as I watched the retreating enemy to see every man, every officer, take off cap and give "Three Cheers for General Custer!" It is the first time I ever knew of such a demonstration except in the case of General McClellan. I certainly felt highly flattered. The commander is a graduate of West Point long before my time, and yet as enthusiastic over your boy as if he were a youth of eighteen.

After the battle I heard "By G—d Custer is a brick!" "Custer is the man for us!" And other expressions somewhat rough but hearty.

Gen'l. Merritt was present during part of the engagement, but never gave me an order or suggestion, even. The battle was called by many "the handsomest fight of the war," because fought on open ground, and successful.

[21 August 1867]

Darling little one, Yesterday, the 9th, was a glorious day for your Boy. He signalized his accession to his new command by a brilliant victory. . . . My new command is perfectly enthusiastic.

[October 1864]

My darling sunbeam—I cannot tell you how hard and earnestly I have worked to make this expedition a success. I have been, not only Commanding Officer, but also Guide, among other things. . . . I have the proud satisfaction of knowing not only that our explorations have exceeded the most sanguine expectations but that my superior officers will be pleased with the extent and thoroughness of these. . . .

I have reached the hunter's highest round of fame. . . . I have killed my Grizzly.

[August 1874][11]

The last letter ever written by Custer to Libbie, on 22 June 1876, was in precisely the same vein.

My Darling . . . . I send you an extract from Gen'l. Terry's official order, knowing how keenly you appreciate words of commendation and confidence in your dear Bo: "It is of course impossible to give you any definite instructions in regard to this movement, and, were it not impossible to do so, the Department Commander places too much confidence in your zeal, energy and ability to impose upon you precise orders which might hamper your action when nearly in contact with the enemy." Your devoted boy, Autie.[12]

In addition to such passages extolling his courage, energy, and military effectiveness, there are others in which Custer emphasized his (and his men's) virtues, especially of restraint.

Oh, I forgot to tell you: I have not uttered a single oath or blasphemed, even in thought, since I saw you, so strictly have I kept my resolution.

[March 1865]

I am prouder and prouder of the 7th, Libbie; not an officer or man of my command has been seen intoxicated since the expedition left Fort Rice.

[June 1873]

We reach Lincoln about the 31st. There has been no drunkenness, no card-playing on this trip.

[August 1874][13]

Custer's tendency to show off was by no means limited to his letters. Libbie relates a revealing incident. One day she and Custer had gone riding, accompanied by an orderly.

Those eyes [of the orderly] were wide with terror one day, when our horses were going full tilt, and the General with one powerful arm, lifted me out of my saddle and held me poised in the air for a moment. . . . The moment I was thus held aloft was an hour in uncertainty, but nothing happened, and it taught me to prepare for sudden raids of the commanding officer after that.[14]

Apart from their letters to one another, the record of Custer and Libbie's married life tells a great deal in itself. Probably the outstanding feature is the extent to which, for a military couple, they were together. This was certainly a matter of mutual wishes, but there is no doubt that it was extremely important to Custer. Even at the start of their marriage during the Civil War, Libbie (by Custer's arrangement) spent more time at advanced positions than was usual for an army wife. The most striking example, however, of Custer's need to see his wife as much as possible is afforded by the events of the Hancock expedition leading to his court-martial, for it seems reasonably clear that Custer's dependence on Libbie's presence clouded his judgment. Libbie stirred up his wishes to see her by playing upon his sympathy, as in a letter of 26 April 1867.

I know you are wondering why this letter is cut up so. Well, I began to try to cut out the tearstains, for I know I ought not to send such doleful letters, but I had to give up the cutting as a bad job, for I would soon have had nothing at all to give to the messenger.[15]

Yet Custer did not require such stimulation, for his need to be with Libbie was so great that he was planning for her to join him even before he received her message.

I marched one hundred and fifty miles in four days and a half, an average of over thirty-three miles a day. One night we were marching till daylight.

[20 April 1867]

If Indian hostilities should be the result of this expedition, and I am sent off independently during the summer, as I am at present, I believe you can go with me. The fatigues of the march will be all that you will have to contend against, and these will not be greater than those encountered in going through Texas. As for overtaking the Indians, it is almost an impossibility. Our horses cannot endure the marching their ponies can, fed upon nothing but prairiegrass.

[22 April 1867][16]

Later on the same campaign Custer wrote from the forks of the Republican River:

You cannot imagine my anxiety regarding your whereabouts, for the reason that, if you are now at Wallace, you can join me in about six days, and we can be together all summer. . . . I am expected to keep the Indians quiet on the Platte route to Denver. They are pretty well scared. . . . Tell me when you can be at Wallace, and I will send a squadron there for you; although we sometimes make thirty-five miles a day, it is not usual.[17]

The conflict of motives within Custer could not be plainer. He is moving his men at exhausting forced marches, yet the experience will not be too much for Libbie; he is supposed to find hostile Indians, yet he will probably not do so, and so it is safe enough for her to accompany the regiment.

Playfulness and whimsy were also characteristic of the Custers' marriage and household. On one occasion, for example, having shaved off his cavalryman's mustache, Custer mailed it in an envelope to Libbie.[18] The two were given to exuberance, and Custer to boisterousness, pranks and joking, and outbursts of energy. Libbie wrote:

From the first days of our marriage General Custer celebrated each order to move with wild demonstrations of joy. His exuberance of spirits always found expression in some boyish pranks before he could set to work seriously to prepare for duty. As soon as the officer announcing the order to move had disappeared, all sort of wild hilarity began. I had learned to take up a safe position on top of the table—that is, if I had not already been forcibly placed there as a spectator. The most disastrous result of the proceedings was possibly a broken chair, which the master of ceremonies would crash, and perhaps throw into the kitchen by way of informing the cook that good news had come.

There were picnics and excursions, and there were many romantic evenings.

An ineffaceable picture remains with me even now of those lovely camps, as we dreamily watched them by the fading light of the afternoon. The general and I used to think there was no bit of color equal to the delicate blue line of smoke which rose from the campfire, where the soldiers' suppers were being cooked. The effect of light and shade, and the varying tints of that perfect sky, were a great delight to him. The mellow air brought us sounds that had become dear by long and happy association—the low notes of the bugle in the hands of the musician practicing the calls; the click of the currycomb as the soldiers groomed their horses.[19]

There was a quaint good humor in bed. Libbie wrote of a stormy night:

> My husband, accustomed to the pyrotechnic display of the elements, slept soundly through the early part of the storm. But lightning "murders sleep" with me, and consequently he was awakened by a conjugal joggle, and on asking, "What is it?" was informed, "It lightens!" Often as this statement was made to him in his sudden awakenings, I do not remember his ever meeting it with any but a teasing, laughing reply, like: "Ah! indeed; I am pleased to be informed of so important a fact. This news was quite unexpected," and so on, or, "When, may I inquire, did you learn this?"[20]

Relatives and close friends were much in evidence. Tom Custer was a fixture in the Custer home; it was not a *ménage à trois* in the usual sense of the phrase, but Tom was always there. Later Custer's sister Maggie and her husband, Lieutenant Calhoun, were in the intimate family circle. Frequently the Custers would invite girlfriends of Libbie to stay with them, and Libbie would try her hand at matchmaking. As was usual and necessary in frontier settings, there was much home entertainment. Libbie would play the piano, with Custer often turning the pages of her music. There were games—Custer enjoyed humorous charades—and there was dancing.

There were always many pets in the household.

> Our tents were usually a menagerie of pets: the soldiers, knowing General Custer's love for them, brought him everything that they could capture. The wolf was the only one in the collection to which I objected. . . . The dogs, of course, ran in and out at will; no one ever thought of repressing them.

> At one time the general tamed a tiny field mouse and kept it in a large, empty inkstand on his desk. It grew very fond of him and ran over his head and shoulders and even through his hair.[21]

There were, however, no children. Early in the marriage Libbie expressed the wish to give Custer a son, but this never came to pass. Custer is also known to have expressed a wish for children—he was always a strong family man. (On one occasion Libbie declined Custer's suggestion that they adopt a young relative of his.) Years afterward Libbie wrote, perhaps somewhat enviously: "The young wife of one of our Seventh Cavalry officers was the occupant of quarters on one side. . . . A swarm of little children prevented her from coming to camp to live, but she consoled herself by the permit her husband received to spend every Saturday night to Monday morning of every week at home."[22] The reason for the couple's infertility is not known. There have, of course, been speculations. Mari Sandoz claimed that the Fort Sill medical records showed Custer and his brother Tom to have received treatment for syphilis in 1868 and 1869. If Custer had at any time had the much commoner gonorrhea and had not been promptly treated, Libbie might have contracted it and been made sterile. However, the Fort Sill records have recently been reexamined, and Sandoz's claim has been demonstrated to be incorrect, at least for the years stated. Lawrence Frost has speculated that "more than likely the problem would be a sterility imposed upon him [Custer] by the trauma of hard riding, a not uncommon occupational hazard in the cavalry."[23]

Sandoz, who interviewed many Plains Indians, also gave credence to the story that Custer fathered a child by a young Cheyenne woman named Mo-nah-se-tah, whom he took prisoner at the Battle of the Washita. There is no question that Mo-nah-se-tah was for a time kept at Fort Supply (and perhaps at Fort Dodge) and that Custer took her along on at least one scout as an interpreter. It is also true that Mo-nah-se-tah bore a child in January 1869 while with Custer's command. However, this birth occurred less than two months after the Washita fight, and there is no record of a second child. On the other hand, it seems possible that Custer and Mo-nah-se-tah (or some other Indian woman) were at some time lovers. In addition to the Cheyenne stories, it is known that Captain Benteen referred to Custer's having been cuckolded at the time of the birth of the Indian girl's baby.[24] Making all due allowance for Benteen's spleen, and realizing that a time distortion or a confusion of identities may have taken place in this tangled story, it appears that some of the officers must have believed that Custer had had sexual contact with an Indian girl in the camp.

Another story about Custer and Libbie in a quite different vein is to the effect that Libbie actually wrote the works published under her husband's name. This, like the story of Custer's fathering Mo-nah-se-tah's child, must be put in the category of gossip. Libbie certainly encouraged Custer to write—as he did her, although she only followed his advice much later. However, Custer's style, as shown in *My Life on the Plains* and elsewhere, is quite different from Libbie's. It does seem likely that Libbie may have corrected or copied his manuscripts, for Custer was a poor speller though a good writer.

Taken all in all, the picture one obtains of the Custers' marriage is a colorful and curious one. Surely husband and wife were well suited to one another and each had great need of the other. On the one hand, the marriage had the qualities of a shared, perpetual adolescence. On the other, there was a good bit of parenting, both of Custer by Libbie and of Libbie by Custer.

TEN

An Analysis of Custer's Personality

WHAT kind of man was Custer? It is the thesis of this book that a fuller understanding of the man can shed further light on the Battle of the Little Big Horn. When one seeks this understanding objectively, without any interest in making of Custer either a hero or a villain, what begins to emerge is the picture of an interesting and moderately complex personality, with specific strengths and weaknesses, personal conflicts and defenses, reacting to the stresses of life in ways which have a certain inner consistency. The characterization and the plot, while the one does not fully explain the other, can yet be seen to belong together.

To begin at the surface, it is not a difficult matter to list Custer's outstanding characteristics. There were, for example, sheer physical energy, athleticism, and hardihood. From his boyhood in which he excelled at games and sports, through the Civil War years, when he was a most strenuous campaigner, and the plains years when he carried out forced marches which left nearly everyone else exhausted, his energy and endurance were unflagging. The athleticism was manifested in Custer's superb if somewhat unconventional horsemanship and in his liking to perform special feats, such as lifting Libbie from her saddle when they were galloping side-by-side and replacing her without a break in the rhythm.

Custer also had remarkable physical courage. This characteristic was mingled with, and quite likely partly dependent upon, his belief in his own good fortune, and yet one sees no reason to question its validity. Custer's men, whatever they may have thought of him otherwise, always admired his valor after he had led them in battle. Custer's talents were shown not only in combat leadership, but perhaps even more in his marvelous ability as a pathfinder, at which, Cyrus Brady said, he was "even better than Fremont."[1]

Although, like Grant, Sheridan, Stonewall Jackson, and other famous military leaders, Custer was never a good student, he was both intelligent and talented. That he did graduate from West Point, in spite of meager preparation and lack of effort, shows a good native intelligence. So also does his writing, which, although conventional and often clichéd, nevertheless still reads well and compares favorably with memoirs written by more sophisticated authors.

To this list of characteristics could be added a sense of fair play, although it was sometimes overridden by other considerations. This attribution will sound strange to many modern ears in view of Custer's having been a generally willing instrument in Sheridan's devastation of the Shenandoah Valley and in what one can now readily perceive to have been a shameful Indian policy. In such activities Custer was a creature of his time, his class, and his geography, yet he was able to see, more clearly than many of his similarly restricted fellows, some of the deficiencies of Reconstruction and much of the corruption of Grant's War Department. In the matter of the Plains Indians, while agreeing in general with governmental policy, Custer could see the point of view of the hostiles and said as much in print, observing: "If I were an Indian, I often think, I would greatly prefer to cast my lot among those of my people who adhered to the free open plains rather than to submit to the confined limits of a reservation, there to be the recipient of the blessed benefits of civilization with its vices thrown in without stint or measure."[2]

Further, and perhaps more importantly in the present context, Custer was capable in the right circumstances of friendship, loyalty, and love. He was a strong family man. He liked having members of his family with him—Tom, Maggie, his father, and others. He repeatedly sent money from his always limited income to his parents and his brother Nevin. He was loyal to certain eminent figures, such as McClellan and Andrew Johnson, and remained so even when this loyalty was detrimental to his career. He was a loving and certainly for the most part loyal husband, who made a charming woman so proud to be his wife that the memory warmed her heart for more than half a century after his death. He loved pets and was usually surrounded by them. What were the "right" circumstances for Custer to love? The principal ones seem to have been those which would facilitate a sense of identification: an initial great admiration or a sense of possession. It should be added that Custer's love seems to have had a strongly dependent quality; that is, it was a love greatly admixed with need. Custer *needed* to have Libbie close to him, as was clearly shown on the Hancock expedition and in the whole pattern of their married life. He *needed* to have Brother Tom with him, as well as other relatives and close friends. Often this need coincided with the needs and even the best interests of these others, but if, as on the Hancock expedition, it did not, Custer's sense of need was likely to prevail.

There are qualifications to be placed upon others of his personality assets. For example, courage, athleticism, and hardihood can be carried to such an extent as to transcend their adaptive value and become swagger and bravado. Some of Custer's famous charges during the Civil War were not well thought out; sometimes other tactics would have produced better results. Similarly, there were episodes in Custer's nonmilitary life in which a display of reckless courage served no realistically adaptive purpose. For example, once during a buffalo hunt Custer ran in and hamstrung a bull buffalo with his knife and dispatched it with his pistol.[3] This caricaturelike exaggeration of traits conventionally associated with virility appears to be related to Custer's spoken and written exaggeration of his accomplishments. Although they were often considerable achievements, his self-aggrandizement reached the point of almost continuous bragging. In letters to his parents, to his sister Lydia Ann, to Libbie, and to others, this feature is conspicuous. The cavalry charge was not merely successful, but the greatest ever made; the expedition was not just carried out well, but superlatively well; the forced march was not merely rapid, but astoundingly fast; the country to be scouted was not partially unexplored, but never before seen by white men. Similarly, Custer's horses were marvels of sagacity; his dogs were unequaled in bravery. And, of course, the Seventh Cavalry was the greatest fighting unit in the entire country.

What emerges clearly from all of these details is that Custer, for all his toughness, courage, and endurance, was in certain respects a highly vulnerable man. His principal weakness appears to have been in the regulation of his self-esteem. Throughout his adult life, Custer seems to have depended to an unusual degree upon a flow of recognition, admiration, and praise from other persons. Whether it came from Lydia Ann or Libbie, whether Pleasonton or Sheridan, the pattern is unmistakably there. Although this need was coupled with strong ambition, the two features are not identical; it is quite possible, in other words, for a person to have high ambitions and yet not to feel humiliated or depleted if at times the ambitions are not being gratified or the achievements recognized. Custer's ambitions—he wanted glory and renown, particularly military glory and renown—were indeed strong.

For those interested in a diagnosis, it can be argued that Custer exemplified a form of *narcissistic personality disorder* (coming close to representing the old diagnostic concept of *phallic narcissist* as described by Wilhelm Reich).[4] As Heinz Kohut and others have shown, the development of a wholesome and stable sense of, and regard for, the self can be somewhat independent of other aspects of personality development.[5] Thus it is possible for a person's self-esteem regulation to be less than autonomous without his being in any way out of touch with reality or incapable of major personal and vocational accomplishments. The key feature in one major variety of this disorder (the *mirror personality)* is the one so evident in Custer's life: the subject requires a nearly constant reflection back upon himself from others of favorable opinions. In Custer's case the narcissistic personality disorder appears to have been of medium intensity. It was obvious enough to have offended many persons (notably Benteen, but also Stanley, Cooper, and others), but it was mild enough to have permitted friendships, camaraderie, and even love, in which healthier elements played a significant part.

A diagnostic phrase seldom can sum up a personality, and certainly "narcissistic personality disorder" does not sum up Custer's. There appear to be three principal items of data, three areas or aspects of Custer's life story, which suggest that a more complex interpretation is needed. These are the material regarding Custer's earliest years; certain specific personality features, including particularly

Custer's humorousness; and what is known of Terry's critical strategy conference aboard the *Far West*.

A consideration of the known facts regarding Custer's infancy and early childhood has, in the present connection, both negative and positive aspects. The negative aspect is that essentially nothing is known of his first two years save that he was much loved by both parents. The idea of any sort of psychic trauma during this period—a necessary postulate for the development of a severe narcissistic personality—remains hypothetical and therefore cannot be used to explain later characteristics. The positive aspect is that a good deal *is* known of Custer's childhood after this early period, and these data lend themselves to formulations deriving from later (oedipal) issues.

It would be incorrect, in this connection, to make a great deal of the fact that Custer had some strong and long-lasting friendships, for, in favorable circumstances, this characteristic has been shown to obtain in individuals who may be accurately summed up as narcissistic personalities. Such persons are certainly capable of behavior which is both impressive and ingratiating, and when various Custer biographers report, for example, that Custer made a strongly favorable impression upon the Grand Duke Alexis of Russia, the information does not affect the diagnosis. On the other hand, the number and warmth of Custer's friendships are atypical of a seriously narcissistic personality. So are their heartiness and playfulness. Custer's humorousness deserves additional comments, though here again one should discriminate. A sense of humor which delights in practical jokes, especially at others' expense, is compatible with a serious degree of narcissistic difficulty. Custer did indeed enjoy practical jokes—including, however, some at his own expense. More important in the present context is the fact that Custer's sense of humor often had a *whimsical character*. The dialogue Libbie quotes about thunderstorms and Custer's known liking for charades are examples of this aspect. The point is that whimsy involves a lightness and, at times, an unselfconsciousness which would be quite out of keeping for a serious narcissistic difficulty.

The decisive element in the present discussion is perhaps the conference aboard the *Far West* and what followed it. This episode will be further discussed later on in this chapter, but it should be recalled that there is good reason to believe that it was at this point that Terry informed Custer that he would have an independent command. It is certainly known that Terry was kind, supportive, and considerate of Custer during the conference and in the letter of instructions which followed. It is, moreover, entirely clear that Custer was aware of and appreciated Terry's goodwill. That there was a change in Custer's mood and manner following the *Far West* conference is generally agreed to: Custer became temporarily irritable and depressed. It is simply impossible to trace this alteration to any sort of narcissistic injury, for there was none.

What one is left with then, in this attempt at understanding Custer, is that the broad diagnosis of narcissistic personality disorder is applicable, but far from being the whole story. It is virtually impossible to trace this alteration to any sort of narcissistic injury, for there is no evidence to support the idea. One reaches firmer ground in returning to Custer's other demonstrable personal characteristics, particularly certain specific features of his interpersonal relationships. More is known about his relationships with men than with women, and, as previously suggested, they involved an interesting dichotomy. Custer seems in general to have divided older men into two categories. The first comprised prominent men, men who were typically considerably older than Custer and in positions of authority. Examples were Judge Bacon and Generals Kearny, McClellan, Pleasonton, and Sheridan. The second category comprised men who were only a few years older than Custer or whose authority was limited, usually being only slightly greater than his own. Examples were several of Custer's unit commanders during the Civil War, such as Merritt, and Colonel Stanley of the Yellowstone expedition. (Terry, as will be shown later, did not fit well into either category, and this circumstance seems to have created special difficulties for Custer.)

Custer's reactions to men in the first category differed strikingly from those to men in the second. With the self-confident, high-ranking, appreciably older man, Custer's typical reaction was prompt, loyal, vigorous, but rather passive (in the sense of involving almost automatic compliance). With the somewhat older man of only slightly higher authority and rank, Custer's typical reaction was to take the bit in his teeth and move on his own, not so much disobeying as disregarding the other's commands or expectations if they restricted his own activities. With younger men, or with men who were a little older but his junior in rank, the situation was somewhat different, but again involved a dichotomy. If the subordinate, though junior in rank, were a bit older than Custer, and if earlier he had held higher commands or a high brevet rank, there was likely to be trouble. Examples were Cooper, West, Reno, and Benteen. If the subordinate were junior both in age and in rank, or if he were older but had never held appreciably higher rank and was not pretentious, things would go well, particularly if he became a Custer admirer, as in the cases of Keogh, Moylan, Calhoun, Yates, and of course Tom Custer.

Custer's relationships with women perhaps tended also to involve a dichotomy. If they were members of his family—his mother, Lydia Ann, Libbie, Maggie—they were idealized. If not, they were still treated kindly, and if Custer perceived them as equal to or of a higher social status than himself, they were likely to be treated with gallantry and respect. Otherwise—but here the record becomes too vague to speak in other than a highly tentative way. Custer could write suggestively of showgirls in New York; it was rumored that he had acquired syphilis; he seems to have been, at the very least, much attracted to Mo-nah-se-tah. These are merely hints that there may have been a different type of woman for Custer, one who was regarded essentially as a sexual object. The idea of such a dichotomy is perhaps reinforced by Custer's rebuking Libbie for having written him passionate love letters.

To all these descriptive and diagnostic statements about Custer's personality and behavior should be added one other point, of an inferential nature. The basis for the inference is a series of rash and self-destructive acts which one cannot help noticing in any close look at Custer's career. Among these are his becoming conspicuously drunk on his first triumphant return to Monroe as an officer and a gentleman; his conspicuous adherence to President Johnson while he was a major general and the president's influence was at a low ebb; his obvious violation of orders on the Hancock expedition, his first real chance to establish himself in his new role as acting commander of the Seventh Cavalry; his taking an unprecedentedly long eight-months leave of absence in 1871, when his advancement in the military already seemed problematic; and his striking out rashly at Secretary of War Belknap in early 1876, an action which, until Terry's intervention, cost him the leadership of his regiment. The list is impressive, and there may well have been additional instances of a similar nature, for the fact is that, despite a number of effective and celebrated performances, Custer did not receive a promotion during the last ten years of his life.

How is one to account for these episodes of self-injurious behavior? To an extent each has its own set of explanations. To an extent also each may be accounted for as merely a by-product of an habitual carelessness or heedlessness. Yet the pattern is so strong that it is clearly a permissible inference, that somewhere deep inside Custer was an obscure, unconscious sense of guilt which contributed to the pattern of his repeatedly spoiling success by some rash act. One is playing the odds in making such a deduction: generally speaking an unconscious sense of guilt is the likeliest motive for such behavior. There is some evidence to support the deduction, and perhaps the clearest portion of it is Custer's amazing string of not guilty pleas to the various charges and specifications of his court-martial. It is a case of betraying by denial, of protesting too much.

Given the preceding cross-sectional picture of Custer's personality, one now may attempt to trace the longitudinal or developmental story. Here the evidence is limited, as so often is the case in the study of historical figures. Yet on the whole more is known of Custer's formative years than is known of those of many distinguished contemporaries, so that while it is sometimes necessary to resort to inferences, there usually is a basis upon which to judge their plausibility and internal consistency.

Surely one of the most specific and significant features of Custer's earliest years must have been his situation in the family. Because both parents had been widowed and had brought children by their first marriage into the new household, and because Maria Custer's first and second pregnancies by Emanuel resulted in infants who died soon after birth, the sturdy boy-child George Armstrong found himself in a unique position. He was at once the favorite child in an established family, and, for nearly three years, the only living child of his parents' union. During his childhood he must usually have been able to prevail in any dispute with his older half-siblings, as well as, generally speaking, with his younger full siblings. Yet, after having been the natural focus of attention for almost the first three years of his existence, he was faced with Nevin's birth. It seems highly probable that this event (aggravated by Nevin's sickliness) constituted a trauma for Autie. The arrival of younger siblings is normally difficult for the small child to master psychologically, but usually it is mastered satisfactorily in time. In this instance, however, there were a number of special features which any child psychiatrist would a priori consider highly likely to make the problem especially severe. The special and prolonged indulgence of Custer's earliest years would have made him vulnerable to a change, and the change was quite probably more than usually pronounced because of the poor health of the new arrival, which demanded an exceptionally large amount of maternal attention.

It has for a long time been known that a frequent response of children to an emotional threat is to regress to an earlier level of development. As a three-year-old boy, Custer must have been strongly inclined to do this. Such a regression would involve two aspects: a regression of impulses and a closely related disturbance in the inner mechanisms for the regulation of self-esteem. It has already been shown that Custer did indeed have a rather severe problem in the latter respect, needing more or less constant supplies of admiration by his associates in order to maintain a feeling of well-being. The tendency toward regressive impulses—that is, toward impulses typical of a younger child, so-called oral and anal impulses—can easily be demonstrated. The careless, undisciplined nature of Custer's scholastic efforts in his early years is one bit of evidence. His record of demerits at West Point, almost all of which were incurred for carelessness in attire, messiness in his room, tardiness, and lack of discipline, is further evidence. Then too, there were the oral impulses toward drinking, smoking, swearing, and gambling, all common enough in a young soldier and yet a little out of the ordinary in a young man of strict religious upbringing. And, finally, there was the slight stammer, which is usually an indication of a psychological problem in the very early, preoedipal years.

It is to be noted, however, that all these impulses were overshadowed, even from the first, by behavior at a slightly more advanced level. Furthermore, they were resisted and eventually almost completely mastered. Putting to one side for the moment Custer's intellectual development (respectable) and his physical development (remarkable), and concentrating solely on his instinctual (psychosexual) development, the impression one receives is not that of a very small child, but rather that of a child of three or four years trying very hard to be a big boy. One image that comes to mind is of such a child riding by on his tricycle and calling, "Look, Mommie! No hands!" This concept, that of a small boy trying hard not to be a baby, striving to be like a bigger boy (as this would be visualized at age three or four), goes far to explain some of the features of Custer's later life. It looks as if Custer unconsciously continued trying to be a big boy all of his life, long after chronological boyhood was past.

One can see fairly readily how the self-esteem problem fits in with all this. What its original source might have been—such a problem usually has its remotest origin in the first two years of life—cannot be guessed with assurance, let alone confirmed. However, the postulated regressive tendency would go a long way toward increasing Custer's vulnerability. That is to say, the existence of strong tendencies to feel and behave like a tiny child, however much the tendencies were repressed and resisted, would produce some shame and probably some guilt.

One of the key features in any personality consists of the psychological maneuvers, particularly the deep-seated, unconscious ones (so-called defense mechanisms) by means of which anxiety is warded off and an equilibrium is maintained. In Custer's case, it is postulated that the principal anxiety (unconscious) came from his tendency to regress to the passive situation of infancy or to the more aggressive but still largely ineffectual situation of the second year of life. The principal defense mechanism used to ward off regression and its attendant anxiety seems very clearly to have been *reaction-formation*. (This mechanism, as elucidated by Sigmund Freud and Anna Freud, may be defined, though not explained, as the psychological device whereby an original attitude or set of feelings is replaced in consciousness by the opposite attitude or feelings.)[6] In other words, tendencies toward assuming the passive, help-seeking, nourishment-needing attitude typical of the first year, or the messy, unregulated attitude typical of the second year, were turned into the confident, aggressive attitude typical of an outward-directed older boy. As is usually the case when a defense mechanism is used unconsciously, there is a tendency toward exaggeration in the resulting attitudes. Thus independence, confidence, and socially acceptable aggression tend to become flamboyance and belligerence. The youthfully careless Custer became almost a fanatic about discipline as an adult, at least in others. Instead of becoming a moderate drinker, he became a teetotaler. These shifts also indicate the use of reaction-formation.

The anecdote of young Autie and his father after the painful tooth extraction illustrates the working of such a mechanism perfectly. The anxiety-ridden situation, which would naturally tend to produce crying and clinging, results instead in the belligerent "You and me can whip all the Whigs in Ohio!" Similarly, ten or twelve years later, the heckling during the spelling bee—and spelling was always one of Autie's weaknesses—resulted neither in giving in nor in quietly redoubled effort, but rather in smashing out at the heckler through a pane of glass.

The exaggerated quality of Custer's daring, his tendency to bravado and unnecessary heroics, is suggestive of the use of reaction-formation in a rather specific way, producing what is often called a *counterphobic reaction*. In such a reaction the subject does not show or even consciously feel the anxiety or fear which would be natural, but instead rushes to meet or even seeks out the dangerous situation. One cannot, of course, be certain, but some of Custer's actions seem to fall in this category. Sometimes a cavalry charge is not the ideal way of handling a military situation, and a bull buffalo is more effectively handled with rifle shots than with a knife and pistol. Custer's apparent boyhood water phobia, although perhaps mild, is also interesting in this connection. It indicates a tendency, ordinarily not given expression, to react in a phobic manner; it was one instance in which the habitual defense mechanism did not work. (The specific nature of this phobia, having to do with immersion in water, would be of potential significance to the psychoanalyst. Water, in dreams and in neurotic symptoms, usually has the unconscious significance of a return to the mother's womb, and thus implies strong passive tendencies. Such an interpretation here, while of course unproven, is consonant with what has been suggested about the infantile passive tendencies against which Custer seems to have struggled with general success.)

Custer's father and mother were of course highly important figures in his earliest environment. The impact of Emanuel upon his famous son must have been complex. The physically powerful, loud-talking father must have been awesome to a very small boy. On the other hand, a boy as smart as Custer would soon have found that this impressive father in reality had feet of clay. Not only was Emanuel incapable of maintaining discipline within his family, but he was an unimpressive, even insignificant figure outside the hamlet of New Rumley. Conscious disillusionment would be inevitable, and it is fair to suppose unconscious resentment.

Custer's mother, on the other hand, while she very likely inadvertently changed from being a completely indulgent mother in his earliest years to being a somewhat frustrating one a bit later on, seems to have remained the power behind the throne. She had slightly higher social pretensions than Emanuel; she wanted Custer to achieve (in particular, to be a scholar), and it seems to have been from her that Custer derived his vaunting ambition. She was a strong conscience figure always, as was her deputy, Lydia Ann. Moreover, she tended, at least in her later years, to control through a show of weakness which stimulated guilt feelings. It is no wonder that Custer sought and found a wife who, though like his mother in her admiration of and ambition for him, was in almost all other respects quite different. Nor is it any wonder that, with his mother-fixation, Custer treated Libbie in many ways like a mother—most strikingly in his constant need of her presence.

In tracing Custer's history, one can scarcely avoid being struck by the cyclic nature of his fortunes.

Ups	Downs
(1838–42) Favored one in family for almost three years	(1842–?) Displacement of mother's attention and concern by Nevin's birth and sickly condition
(1844–?) Boyhood and adolescent successes	(1849–?) Realization, probably from life in Monroe, that he and his family were of low socioeconomic status
(1857) Appointment to West Point	(1857–61) Almost failing out or getting dismissed for demerits
(1861–65) Outstanding successes during the Civil War (this period could be subdivided into a series of successes and minor reverses)	(1866) Demotion to captain's rank and pay

(1866) Offer of generalcy in the army of Juarez	(1866) Denial of leave of absence; inability to accept generalcy
(July 1866) Lieutenant colonelcy; assignment to Seventh Cavalry	(October 1867) Court-martial after Hancock expedition
(November 1868) Battle of the Washita; national recognition	(1869–73) Repercussions about Major Elliott; promotions go to others; denial of West Point superintendency; Sturgis made colonel of the Seventh; thoughts of resigning, but failure to get civilian position; low prestige assignment in Elizabethtown
(1874) Black Hills expedition; publication of *My Life on the Plains*	(Sept. 1875–Apr. 1876) Involvement in Belknap impeachment; loss of command of the Seventh
(May 1876) Terry's successful intervention	

There is no clear rhythm to these oscillations. There is, however, a slight though by no means regular tendency for them to increase in magnitude. Custer was never, until his death, more famous than after the Battle of the Washita or his discovery of gold. He was deeper in trouble than usual at his court-martial and deepest of all at the time of the Belknap affair. The Battle of the Little Big Horn can in a sense be seen to be a logical last term in this progression in that Custer reached his zenith and his nadir in this action: he met his death, yet he became immortal.

A cyclic pattern such as Custer's life reveals is wholly likely to have had more than one cause. Most careers have their ups and downs, and this was more than usually the case with military careers of the 1860s and 1870s in view of such factors as the expansion and shrinkage of the army and the heavy influence of political concerns. Yet the oscillations in Custer's fortunes seem to have begun before the war and to have been unusual in their frequency and amplitude. It therefore seems probable that certain characteristics of Custer's personality were contributing to the pattern. One of these characteristics seems reasonably clear: Custer reacted to a sense of humiliation (and probably shame) with a surge of glory-seeking activity designed to wipe out the negative emotions. The other is less clear; it is, however, consistent with all the known facts, and if present would serve to explain behavior the motivation for which would otherwise remain exceedingly obscure. This factor is the previously hypothesized sense of guilt to which Custer seems to have reacted with actions tending to be self-destructive. A self-perpetuating cycle was thus created. A sense of humiliation and shame led to vigorous efforts at achievement, restoring feelings of well-being; after a time, a sense of guilt led to self-destructive behavior. The resulting loss of status gave fresh stimulation to the sense of humiliation and shame and the cycle started over.

Naturally this formulation is tentative. What one is sure of is that Custer's life did show significant oscillations, and one can also reasonably say that Custer's own behavior contributed appreciably to many of the ups and downs. Taking the achievement side of the ledger, one sees quite clearly that Custer did, for example, develop his physical skills and did exert leadership among his companions as a boy; he did create a favorable impression upon Representative Bingham which brought him his West Point appointment; he did show great valor and thus win renown in the Civil War, and so on. Yet one sees with equal clarity that Custer did, for example, almost get dismissed from West Point for undisciplined behavior and did repeatedly come very close to getting dropped for poor grades due to lack of study; he did violate military orders on the Hancock expedition, bringing about his court-martial; he did neglect to make an all-out effort to find Major Elliott, and so on. In other words, while granting the existence of external factors in Custer's oscillations in status, one cannot dismiss the evidence that to a considerable extent his character was his destiny—not in any simplistic sense, but in the sense that specific elements in his personality influenced his behavior, at times in one direction and at times in another. The question then arises: what is the likeliest—not the only possible—configuration of these personality factors? The shame-guilt formulation appears to fit the requirements of the situation, but it needs closer examination.

Locating the remote, underlying sources of the humiliation-shame potential in Custer appears to be reasonably well supported by the data. Identifying the remote, underlying sources of the guilt potential is more speculative, but it seems reasonable to infer that Custer's unconscious guilt feelings sprang in the first instance (and were thereafter sustained) by his awareness that he was supplanting and surpassing his father and all of his half-siblings. As a small boy he was his mother's favorite, and, while remaining so in later years, he quickly moved many notches above Emanuel in financial standing, social standing, and renown, clearly replacing him as head of the family. This father-related guilt would very likely have been considerably enhanced by Emanuel's generosity in selling his farm to launch Custer on his West Point career. Another possible source of unconscious guilt feelings—and this inference is based primarily upon the naturalness and frequency of such developments—may well have been an unconscious resentment of Nevin's privileged and unassailable position, which apparently commanded assistance and support through weakness.

To produce a pattern of high and low points such as I have been describing, it is usual for the original conflicts, whatever they may have been, to have been reinforced in the individual's later life. It is not that the original conflicts become inactive merely because they become more or less repressed, but that typically they require further stimulation by current events if they are to be strongly effective in determining adult behavior. Here again it is not possible to prove that experiences in Custer's adulthood did act in this way, but it is easy to point to some which could well have done so.

Two elements in Custer's post–Civil War life well calculated to stimulate shame and humiliation, whether consciously recognized or not, were his inability to beget children and his failure to receive promotion after 1866. An element well calculated to stimulate a sense of guilt, whether recognized or not, was his not having rescued, or made a sustained effort to rescue, young Major Elliott. This last speculation is strongly supported by the episode in which Custer heard Benteen's admission to having written the highly critical letter without carrying through his avowed intention of retaliating. In view of Custer's physical courage, habitual self-righteousness, and characteristic, vigorous defensiveness of his own dignity, his inaction on this occasion certainly seems to bespeak a guilty conscience.

It is postulated that there were two principal conflict areas which were more or less chronically active in Custer, and which, it may now be added, seem to have been especially active as he moved into the series of events leading to the Last Stand. There was, first, the broad general area which has just been presented, *the cyclic pattern,* with its shame-avoiding, glory-seeking component and its other component, the unrecognized guilt feelings and their tendency to lead to self-destructive conduct. The second, demonstrably clear, conflict area was that of *Custer's relationship to older men,* particularly his superiors. He tended to respond with loyal and even somewhat passive compliance to the person well above him in status and rank, whereas he tended to respond with energetic, somewhat contemptuous, and self-seeking activity to the person immediately above him, particularly if that person were lacking in self-assurance or dignity.

Custer's childhood situation goes a long way toward explaining his dichotomizing his superiors into those who could be ignored and those who must be obeyed. It also seems to explain his problem with older subordinates. The formulation appears to be as follows: if Custer unconsciously identified an older man with his older male siblings, he felt quite safe in having his own way with him, for this must have been a well-established pattern during all the years of his early childhood. The same would be true if he identified him with the financially and socially ineffectual father of his middle childhood and later life. If, on the other hand, he unconsciously identified the man with the physically powerful father as perceived in his earliest years (or perhaps with the morally powerful mother), then the only course would be compliance and submission. It was the peculiarities of Custer's formative early years—his extraordinary position among his half-siblings and his having had a father who was impressive for a short time and thereafter a disappointment—which were almost certainly the basis for these special characteristics of Custer's relationships to men.

Both the shame-guilt cycle and the problem with older men seem to have contributed to the events of 1876. The two conflict areas were not unrelated, since Custer may well have been unconsciously ashamed of his father and unconsciously guilty at having supplanted him. The whole sequence began with Custer's having struck out rashly, although not without justification, at Secretary Belknap, at the president's brother, and by implication at Grant himself. Throughout most of Custer's career, Grant would clearly have belonged in the first category of older men figures. However, his tarnished reputation and diminishing power may well have created at least an unconscious ambiguity in Custer's mind which led to recklessness. In his keen distress at Grant's devastating counterstroke, Custer uncharacteristically turned for succor to a figure who ordinarily would have been in the second category. Terry, however, did not really fit Custer's stereotype of immediate superior officer. He was too cultured, too well educated, and too dignified. Above all, he was neither petty, given to rivalry, nor willing to curry favor with superiors at Custer's expense. (Terry was not self-sacrificing; he really considered Custer to be the best man to lead the Seventh Cavalry, if not the expedition.) He was kind and he exerted himself actively on Custer's behalf. There is no question that Custer owed his reinstatement as leader of the Seventh entirely to Terry. Custer's ambivalence in the situation is exceedingly clear. First there was the conversation with Colonel Ludlow, in which Custer expressed his definite intention of "swinging clear" of Terry and acting in the field as he would see fit. Then there was the conversation with Terry in Libbie's presence, in which Custer expressed his admiration for and loyalty to Terry. The first incident is unmistakable evidence of the rebellious attitude; the second displays the compliant.

During the preliminary stages of the expedition, from its organization to Terry's giving his subordinate commanders their final orders, there was further evidence of Terry's benevolent attitude toward Custer. Perhaps the most obvious example is to be found in Terry's permitting Mark Kellogg to accompany the expedition and, in particular, Custer's regiment. In view of Sherman's position, Terry's decision could have had only one meaning, that of indulging Custer and helping him in his effort to reestablish his reputation. Terry was not a glory-seeker; he was quietly efficient, bent on getting the job done. Further evidence is afforded by Terry's offering the Gatling guns or Brisbin's cavalry battalion. The decisive moment in this whole psychological sequence involving Terry and Custer surely seems to have occurred during the strategy conference on board the *Far West* on the afternoon of 21 June, when Terry evidently revealed to Custer that he would be accompanying Colonel Gibbon and not Custer. It had been unmistakably Sherman's (and so Sheridan's) intention that Custer be the one to be closely supervised. The significance of this episode is very strongly suggested by the change in Custer's mood from his customary prebattle state of elation to the quiet, subdued, almost depressed state of mind in which he left the conference.

It is a principal thesis of this study that Terry's behavior upset Custer's habitual and somewhat stereotyped modes of response to men and left him in an unaccustomed position of uncertainty between a rebellious, but usually effective, outward-directed aggression and dominance of his situation and a compliant, partially passive, attitude with a built-in element of doubt. It is also postulated that Terry's behavior simultaneously influenced Custer's other neurotic sequence, the shame-guilt cycle. Characteristically, at this point in the sequence (that is, having been humiliated by Grant), Custer would have been unequivocally in the shame-dispelling, glory-hunting phase. While he certainly would have acted boldly, if one rated him on past performance one would have to say that he would have acted in a manner likely to bring about a degree of success. In this particular instance, however, it looks as if Terry's extreme kindness (born of strength, not weakness) engendered in Custer an atypical, out-of-phase, self-defeating sense of guilt. This emotion does not seem to have nullified the glory-seeking, shame-avoiding motive, but it certainly seems to have clashed with it.

This emotionally ambivalent situation could not and did not work. It created internal inconsistencies in Custer's decisions, and it appears to have made him less alert in picking up vital cues than was usual for him and than was neccessary if he were to survive. I am not contending that Custer could have produced a victory with the other elements in the situation being what they were, even in his most stable frame of mind. Neither strict adherence to Terry's instructions nor a consistently rebellious but dominant handling of his regiment would have had more than a slim chance of success. However, Custer's conflicted frame of mind contributed significantly to the disaster that overtook him and his command. In part this contribution may have been very general, and thus subtle and hard to demonstrate, but in part it seems to have manifested itself in specific actions, decisions, and failures to make decisions, many of which can be demonstrated. It is postulated that both sets of conflicts were brought to a head. Though the factors involved in each set did not coincide or overlap completely, one can see that the elements of the shame-guilt cycle and those of the dichotomy involving senior authority figures tended to line up (not consciously, of course) in this way: attitudes of rebellion, aggression, shame-avoiding, glory-seeking, exerting dominance, and overcoming obstacles versus attitudes of loyalty, compliance, deference, accepting limitations imposed by the superior, and self-defeating and guilt-ridden attitudes.

If one considers Custer's decisions, actions, and specific inactions from 21 June through 25 June, the greater part of them can be rather readily placed in one or another of two groups, each representing one of these sets of attitudes. Some of the items call for further discussion, but they can be listed as follows:

Rebellious or glory-seeking (shame-avoiding) attitudes	*Compliant or self-defeating (guilt-ridden) attitudes*
Determination to follow the Indian trail, no matter where or how far it led	Declining Brisbin's battalion and the Gatling guns
Ordering the forced march of the last twenty-four hours of the advance	Displaying subdued, quiet manner
Ignoring Tulloch's Creek	Asking advice of his officers in a conciliatory fashion on the first night
Not sending Scout Herendeen to Terry	Failing to scout Little Big Horn valley before sending the regiment into it
	Dividing command into four units just prior to entering probable combat area

Detaching Benteen for the futile scout to the left

Moving the regiment suddenly to attack the Indian village

The final attack with only five companies after seeing the village in its entirety

The last item seems to involve elements of both attitudes.

The least equivocal examples of Custer's rebellious attitude are furnished by his neglecting to scout the headwaters of Tulloch's Creek and to send Scout Herendeen to report to Terry, since these omissions were in clear and direct violation of orders. Rationing the regiment for fifteen days and instructing its officers to be prepared for an even longer pursuit, however, constitute a larger-scale example. As was noted, it is uncertain whether Terry gave Custer specific verbal instructions to be in the valley of the Little Big Horn on 26 June, as was later claimed by Terry's supporters, but it is clear that he envisioned some sort of combined operation and did not for a moment consider Custer's going after the Indians all the way to the Nebraska reservations, as Custer told his officers might be necessary.[7] Other major examples of the rebellious, glory-seeking attitude were Custer's forced pace late in the march, which brought the regiment almost to the divide on the night of 24–25 June, and his decision to cross the divide and move to a daylight attack on the twenty-fifth (although these involved reality factors as well).

An especially clear example of Custer's compliant attitude was his manner of addressing his officers on the first night of the pursuit. The courtesy, restraint, and quietness of this performance were more typical of Terry than of Custer. In other words, Custer was emulating Terry, just as much earlier he had emulated Kearny and Sheridan. Another very clear example is afforded by Custer's sending Benteen on the needless and most costly "scout to the left" after the regiment had crossed the divide and was almost in contact with the enemy. By this order Custer was having Benteen and his battalion, belatedly and unwisely, do approximately what Terry had ordered him to do while marching up the Rosebud.[8] Custer's having declined both Brisbin's cavalry and the Gatling guns presents still another example of self-defeating impulses, since the former would have increased his actual offensive power by up to one-third and the latter would have increased his defensive firepower by perhaps two-thirds. (Here also some reality factors were involved, but they seem inadequate to account for the decisions.)

In addition to the shame-guilt problem and the problem of ambivalence toward senior male figures, Custer had, as has been noted, a significant problem with male figures who were older than he but junior in rank. It was Custer's usual way with them to expect admiration, indulge in bragging, and give short shrift to resistance of any kind. It is clear that Custer's self-esteem requirements often would not permit him to tolerate similar problems in such subordinates. This problem seems also to have been directly relevant to the course and outcome of the Battle of the

Little Big Horn. Custer undoubtedly had rubbed Reno and Benteen the wrong way for a long time. He was intellectually aware of their disaffection, but his narcissism and the conditioning of his early years made him emotionally impervious (or nearly so) to the danger signals coming from them. That Custer may not have been totally impervious is suggested by the appeal he made to his officers on the night of the twenty-second, but in any case it was entirely too late to have reversed this disaffection. Furthermore, Custer may well have underestimated the resentment of Reno and the hatred of Benteen—surely he never considered the possibility that such feelings would interfere with their military duties—because whatever his personal limitations, he was not himself mean, spiteful, underhanded, or given to bearing grudges.

What all these facts add up to is that, in relying upon his principal subordinates to carry out their orders vigorously, faithfully, and perhaps even imaginatively, Custer was clearly overestimating them. I do not mean to say that either Reno or Benteen was consciously so callous and vindictive as to handle his role in a manner which ensured the deaths of Custer and the five companies under his personal command. It would be quite unjustified to think that either officer consciously interpreted the firing heard downriver as indicating that Custer was in serious danger and deliberately refrained from going promptly to his assistance in order to gratify his dislike or hatred of Custer at the probable expense of the lives of the officers and men with him. On the other hand, a reasonably close study of their conduct during the battle, and particularly during the late afternoon of the twenty-fifth, strongly suggests that something caused them to behave in a fashion that was neither loyal nor gallant. One is led to the conclusion that their powerful negative feelings toward Custer caused them to hear less than they normally would have heard, to interpret the situation incorrectly, and to rationalize their inaction.

Lt. (later Gen.) W. S. Edgerly, who was in Weir's company with Reno and Benteen, later epitomized the situation. "We expected immediate orders to advance and I remarked to the 1st Sgt. that we ought to go to the sound of the firing. . . . *Of course we should have gone*."[9]

Notes

PREFACE

1. I later discovered—if I have understood him correctly—that I was anticipated in this conjecture by Edgar I. Stewart in *Custer's Luck,* p. 319.

2. *Psychosomatic Medicine: Its Principles and Applications* (New York: Norton, 1950), pp. 64–68.

3. *Psychoanalytic Review* 54 (Summer 1967):303–28; reprinted in *Montana: The Magazine of Western History* 21 (1971):32–43.

4. *Legend into History,* p. 1.

5. Since 1976, the manuscript collection of the Custer Battlefield Museum has been on permanent loan to the Eastern Montana State University Library, Billings, Montana.

CHAPTER ONE

1. John M. Carroll, *Custer in Periodicals.*

2. For an excellent discussion of the various features of the controversy which has enwrapped Custer and the Battle of the Little Big Horn, see Robert M. Utley, *Custer and the Great Controversy.*

3. As one example of this interest, see John M. Carroll and Byron Price, *Roll Call on the Little Big Horn, 28 June 1876,* a compilation of the military records of every officer in Terry's and Crook's commands as of the date.

4. Utley, *Custer and the Great Controversy,* pp. 155–58.

5. Robert P. Hughes, "The Campaign against the Sioux in 1876," *Journal of the Military Service Institution of the United States* 18 (January 1896): 44: Hughes's article has been reprinted in W. A. Graham, *The Story of the Little Big Horn,* Appendix 1, pp. 1–44.

6. Ibid., pp. 18–20.

7. W. A. Graham, ed., *Abstract of the Official Record of Proceedings of the Reno Court of Inquiry* Harrisburg, Pa.: Stackpole Co., 1954), p. 266 (hereafter *Abstract*). A complete transcript of the original abstract was privately printed by Graham at Pacific Palisades, California, in 1951. The original manuscript, "Proceedings of the Court of Inquiry in the case of Major Marcus A. Reno, concerning his conduct at the Battle of the Little Big Horn River, June 25–26, 1876," is in the National Archives.

8. For the court's conclusion, see *Abstract,* p. 266; for Reno's dismissal from the army, see Carroll and Price, *Roll Call,* p. 86.

9. *Custer and the Epic of Defeat,* pp. 1–2.

10. Charles K. Hofling, "Current Problems in Psychohistory," *Comprehensive Psychiatry* 17 (January-February 1976):227–39.

CHAPTER TWO

1. *Custer's Luck,* pp. 48–49.

2. The provisions of what is known as the Fort Laramie Treaty are in the *Congressional Record,* 57th Cong., 1st sess., *Sen. Doc.* 452, III; 62d Cong., 2d sess., *Sen. Doc.* 719, II. Abstracts of them are

available in Charles J. Kappler, comp. and ed., *Indian Affairs: Laws and Treaties*, 2 vols. (Washington, D.C.: U.S. Government Printing Office, 1904), 2:998–1007.

3. For a thorough presentation of the Black Hills expedition, see Donald Jackson, *Custer's Gold*.

4. Stewart, *Custer's Luck*, pp. 76–80.

5. Ibid., pp. 87–119, 140–58, for a description of the composition and activities of Gibbon's command before it came under the field leadership of General Terry.

6. The telegrams involved in these exchanges are given verbatim in Hughes, "Campaign against the Sioux."

7. The original of Custer's letter to Grant is in the William J. Ghent Papers, Library of Congress.

8. Stewart, *Custer's Luck*, pp. 133–34.

9. Hughes, "Campaign against the Sioux," p. 11.

10. If this telegram had not been sent, Custer probably would have remained confined to Fort Abraham Lincoln and therefore would not have perished at the Little Big Horn. The original is in the William J. Ghent Papers.

11. For a presentation of the exchange of telegrams between Sherman, Sheridan, Terry, and Custer that resulted in the lifting of Custer's arrest and permission for him to return to his regiment, see Hughes, "Campaign against the Sioux," pp. 11–14. The same passage also mentions Custer's tearful plea to Terry and the impulsive remarks to Ludlow cited in the next paragraph.

12. Marguerite Merington, *The Custer Story*, p. 290.

CHAPTER THREE

1. For the strength of the Seventh Cavalry, see John S. Gray, *Centennial Campaign*, p. 97; Edward S. Luce, *Keogh, Commanche, and Custer*, appendices D and E. For the percentage of new enlistments to the Seventh, ibid., pp. 87–88; Stewart, *Custer's Luck*, p. 176.

2. The raw figures often cited regarding "new recruits" or "new enlistments" are misleading, since many such men were veterans of the Civil War. See Stewart, *Custer's Luck*, p. 176; Gray, *Centennial Campaign*, pp. 290–91.

3. Luce, *Keogh, Commanche, and Custer*, appendices D and E.

4. Reno's military career is summarized in Carroll and Price, *Roll Call*, p. 86. For Reno's alcoholism, see *Northwestern Christian Advocate*, 7 September 1904, p. 2, quoted in part in Graham, *Custer Myth*, pp. 338–40.

5. Carroll and Price, *Roll Call*, p. 117. Graham, an admirer of Benteen and an acquaintance of his son, gives an extended discussion of his personality and career and includes a transcription of Benteen's letters to his wife during the 1876 campaign and excerpts from letters about the Seventh Cavalry written later to Theodore W. Goldin (pp. 157–214). Stewart, *Custer's Luck*, p. 169, gives a harsher estimate of Benteen's personality.

6. Carrol and Price, *Roll Call*, p. 124. For Custer's arranging to have Tom placed under his command, see Jay Monaghan, *Custer*, p. 22. For Custer's obtaining a commission for Tom in the Regular Army, see his letter to Libbie Custer of 12 March 1866, quoted in Merington, *Custer Story*, pp. 177–78.

7. For Calhoun's military record, see Carroll and Price, *Roll Call*, p. 121. His marriage to Custer's sister is noted in Merington, *Custer Story*, p. 236. Lawrence A. Frost told me of the second link by marriage to the Custer family. The military careers of Yates, Moylan, and Weir are summarized in Carroll and Price, *Roll Call*, pp. 164, 146, and 162 respectively. Yates's service on Custer's staff is noted in Monaghan, *Custer*, p. 158; Weir's background is mentioned on p. 371. Lawrence A. Frost has told me of Moylan's relationship to Calhoun and close friendship with Custer.

8. For a description of the additional elements in the Dakota column, see Stewart, *Custer's Luck*, pp. 178–82. The Gatling guns are discussed and illustrated in John S. du Mont, *Custer Battle Guns*, pp. 38–39. The military records of the other officers mentioned are given in Carroll and Price, *Roll Call*: Low, p. 74; Kinzie, p. 139; McArthur, p. 75; Sanger, p. 154; and Baker, p. 115; for brief histories of the civilians, see pp. 165–68.

9. Stewart, *Custer's Luck*, pp. 98, 103.

10. Ulysses S. Grant, *Personal Memoirs of U. S. Grant* (New York: Century Co., 1885), pp. 540–41. The principal facts of Terry's career are from *Encyclopedia Americana*, 1969 ed., 26:449; Carroll and Price, *Roll Call*, pp. 158–59. For a brief description of Terry's activities at the taking of Fort Fisher, see John W. Bailey, *Pacifying the Plains: General Alfred Terry and the Decline of the Sioux, 1866–1890* (Westport, Conn.: Greenwood Press, 1979), pp. 6–8.

11. Hughes, "Campaign against the Sioux," pp. 13–14.

12. Edward S. Godfrey, "Diary of Captain E. S. Godfrey, Battle of the Little Big Horn, 1876," pt. 1, entry for 30 May. Pt. 1 of the "Diary" is among the William J. Ghent Papers; pt. 2 is among the Edward S. Godfrey MSS, Library of Congress.

13. Hughes, "Campaign against the Sioux," pp. 15, 16.

14. For Bradley's mission and Terry's decision, described in the following paragraph, see John Gibbon, "Last Summer's Expedition against the Sioux and Its Great Catastrophe," *American Catholic Quarterly Review* (April 1877); reprinted in *Gibbon on the Sioux Campaign of 1876*, of which see esp. p. 19.

15. Fred Dustin, *The Custer Fight*, p. 7.

16. 44 Cong., 1st sess., House Executive Document 184,57, Library of Congress.

17. Gray, *Centennial Campaign*, p. 286.

18. Fred Dustin, *The Custer Tragedy*, p. 62.

19. Secretary of War, *Annual Reports*, 1874–1877, Library of Congress.

20. *Gibbon on the Sioux Campaign*, p. 21.

21. Terry's dispatch was printed in full in the *Philadelphia Inquirer*, 7 July 1876. It is most readily available in Graham, *Story of the Little Big Horn*, pp. 110–14.

22. *Custer's Luck*, p. 244.

23. Hughes, "Campaign against the Sioux," p. 15.

24. Gray, *Centennial Campaign*, p. 143; see also Edward McClernand, "With the Indians and the Buffalo in Montana," *Cavalry Journal* 36 (January-April 1927): 18–24.

25. Dustin, *Custer Tragedy*, p. 93.

26. *Glory-Hunter*, p. 316; see also the long quotation from Godfrey, "Diary," at chap. 3, n. 12.

27. Hughes, "Campaign against the Sioux," pp. 23–26.

28. Graham, *Story of the Little Big Horn*, p. 178. Stewart, *Custer's Luck*, discusses the orders and Custer's execution of them on pp. 250–52. Gray, *Centennial Campaign*, reaches the strong conclusion: "One may quarrel with Custer's judgement, but not his authority to judge. Custer's obedience is therefore neither debatable, nor relevant" (p. 148). It is merely stating a fact to say that the question has long been debated. The psychological relevance of Terry's expectations of Custer, however vaguely phrased, and of Custer's degree of conformity to them, to whatever degree of completeness, seems obvious.

29. Merington, *Custer Story*, p. 307.

30. The matter of the Mary Adams affidavit is one of the more obscure aspects of the Custer story. The document was first quoted in part and brought to public attention in the context of a strong defense of Custer's actions by Gen. Nelson A. Miles in *Personal Recollections and Observations of General Nelson A. Miles*, pp. 197–210. Cyrus Townsend Brady, while preparing material for *Indian Fights and Fighters*, wrote to General Miles on three occasions to ask for further details about the affidavit. Miles did not reply to the first and third letters and answered the second very evasively. Graham devotes an entire chapter of *Custer Myth* to the affidavit. It turned out that the original was in the possession of Custer's widow, and a copy was finally procured for Graham through General Godfrey. This is the version quoted here. Graham pursued the matter and finally concluded on the basis of an article by W. A. Falconer in the *Bismarck Capital* of 25 June 1925—Falconer having been in touch with an officer at Fort Abraham Lincoln when Mrs. Custer received the news of her husband's death—that Mary Adams had stayed behind with her mistress. More recently, Lawrence A. Frost reported having been shown (by the late Col. Brice C. W. Custer, the general's grandnephew) a letter written on 21 June 1876 by Custer's nephew Autie Reed, who died with him at the Little Big Horn (*General Custer's Libbie*, p. 270). Reed referred to Mary Adams's having been on the *Far West*, which means that it would have been physically possible for her to have overheard what the affidavit claims she heard. As I note in the text, however, other improbabilities remain.

31. Hughes, "Campaign against the Sioux," p. 32.

32. All textual references are to Chicago time, about one-and-one-half hours later than sun time. Lt. George Wallace, the expedition's itinerist, used Chicago time in his official account.

33. Quoted in Graham, *Custer Myth*, pp. 134–35. Lt. (later Brig. Gen.) Edward S. Godfrey commanded Company K at the Little Big Horn; his narrative, "Custer's Last Battle," *Century Illustrated Monthly Magazine* 43 (January 1892):358–87, was for a long time considered to be the definitive account. It was republished with some additional material under the same title in *Contributions to the Historical Society of Montana* 9 (1923):141–225. Pertinent excerpts from the *Century* article are reprinted in *Custer Myth*, pp. 125–49, hereafter cited as "Narrative." Over the years

Godfrey developed an increasing antipathy to Reno and a strong devotion to Elizabeth Custer, but Graham considers his descriptive statements to be sound.

34. Du Mont, *Custer Battle Guns,* p. 38.

35. Stewart, *Custer's Luck,* p. 246.

CHAPTER FOUR

1. Dustin, *Custer Tragedy,* p. 88.

2. Stewart, *Custer's Luck,* p. 259.

3. Hughes, "Campaign against the Sioux," pp. 31–32.

4. Dustin, *Custer Tragedy,* pp. 97–98. Terry guaranteed Herendeen a bonus of two hundred dollars for undertaking the ride back. Terry did not have any reliable news of Custer until advance units of Gibbon's column, which Terry accompanied, encountered the sites of the Indian village and the Last Stand, but the importance of communication remained in his mind. Thus he recorded for 26 June: "Before leaving [Tulloch's] creek sent two scouts to communicate with Custer, offering each $200 if they would get through" (Alfred Howe Terry, Diary, 1876–1877, Library of Congress, p. 34).

5. Hughes, "Campaign against the Sioux," p. 29.

6. Godfrey, "Narrative," in Graham, *Custer Myth,* p. 136.

7. *Custer's Luck,* pp. 267–68.

8. *Glory-Hunter,* p. 332. There is a description of the night march in Godfrey, "Narrative," in Graham, *Custer Myth,* p. 136.

9. Hughes, "Campaign against the Sioux," p. 29.

10. *Abstract,* pp. 68 (Moylan), 80 (Herendeen).

11. Ibid., pp. 135 (Benteen), 211 (Reno).

12. T. M. Coughlan, "The Battle of the Little Big Horn: A Tactical Study," *Cavalry Journal* 43 (January-February 1934):16–17; Gray, *Centennial Campaign,* p. 289.

13. Gray, *Centennial Campaign,* pp. 172, 298–303. Gray, of all students of the battle, has made the most careful study of its chronology, and he is usually persuasive when he disagrees with other authorities. The testimony taken at the Reno inquiry is sometimes conflicting and often unreliable. With rare exceptions, this chapter adheres closely to Gray's chronology up to the arrival of the pack train on Reno Hill. For the division of the regiment into battalions, see *Abstract,* p. 157 (Edgerly's testimony); for Benteen's instructions, ibid., pp. 135–36 (Benteen's testimony).

14. *Centennial Campaign,* p. 173.

15. *Abstract,* pp. 135–36.

16. *Custer's Luck,* p. 319.

17. *Abstract,* p. 14 (Wallace).

18. Kuhlman, *Legend into History,* p. 52.

19. *Abstract,* pp. 89 (Hare), 212 (Reno). For the size of Reno's command, see Gray, *Centennial Campaign,* p. 172.

20. *Abstract,* p. 44 (Girard).

21. Ibid., pp. 212–13 (Reno); Stewart, *Custer's Luck,* p. 348.

22. *Abstract,* pp. 212–13 (Reno), 23–24 (Wallace); Stewart, *Custer's Luck,* pp. 348–55.

23. *Saint Paul Pioneer Press,* 18 July 1886, "The Story of Chief Gaul," in Graham, *Custer Myth,* pp. 89–90.

24. Stewart, *Custer's Luck,* pp. 355–57; Gray, *Centennial Campaign,* p. 294. Dr. Henry Porter, a Seventh Cavalry contract surgeon with Reno's battalion, thought that there had been but a single fatality to this point (*Abstract,* p. 63).

25. Gray, *Centennial Campaign,* p. 302.

26. *Abstract,* pp. 82–83 (Herendeen); Graham, *Story of the Little Big Horn,* pp. 42–44; Stewart, *Custer's Luck,* p. 359. For a spirited argument regarding Reno's conduct of this portion of the battle, see W. A. Graham, "My Debate with Captain Carter," in Graham, *Custer Myth,* pp. 301–22.

27. *Abstract,* pp. 65 (Porter), 216 (Reno); Stewart, *Custer's Luck,* pp. 364–72.

28. Stewart, *Custer's Luck,* pp. 372–78; Gray, *Centennial Campaign,* pp. 175–76; Graham, *Story of the Little Big Horn,* pp. 48–49.

29. *Abstract,* p. 136 (Benteen); Stewart, *Custer's Luck,* p. 382.

30. Godfrey, "Narrative," in Graham, *Custer Myth,* p. 138; Stewart, *Custer's Luck,* pp. 382–83.

31. *Abstract,* p. 136 (Benteen): "I came to a burning tepee which contained a dead warrior. A mile or so from that I met a sergeant [Kanipe] coming back with orders to the Commanding Officer of the pack train"; Stewart, *Custer's Luck,* p. 384; Kuhlman, *Legend into History,* p. 83.

32. W. A. Graham, "Come On! Be Quick! Bring Packs!," *Cavalry Journal* 32 (July 1923); reprinted in Graham, *Custer Myth,* pp. 287–94 (the contents of an extended interview with Trumpeter Martin); W. A. Graham, "The Lost Is Found—Custer's Last Message Comes to Light!," *Cavalry Journal* 51 (July–August 1942); reprinted in Graham, *Custer Myth,* pp. 296–300 (the discovery of the actual message written by Cooke).

33. Kuhlman, *Legend into History,* pp. 83, 162–63; Godfrey, "Narrative," in Graham, *Custer Myth,* p. 142.

34. Godfrey,"Diary," entry for 25 June; Stewart, *Custer's Luck,* p. 387.

35. Godfrey, "Narrative," in Graham, *Custer Myth,* p. 141; Stewart, *Custer's Luck,* pp. 388–90; *Abstract,* pp. 138 (Benteen), 160 (Edgerly).

36. Graham, *Story of the Little Big Horn,* pp. 60–61.

37. *Abstract,* pp. 160 (Edgerly), 178 (Godfrey); Graham, *Story of the Little Big Horn,* p. 65.

38. *Abstract,* pp. 55 (Varnum), 178 (Godfrey), 95 (Hare); Stewart, *Custer's Luck,* pp. 395–96.

39. *Abstract,* pp. 160–61 (Edgerly); Godfrey, "Narrative," in Graham, *Custer Myth,* p. 142; Kuhlman, *Legend into History,* pp. 98, 180.

40. Graham, "Come On! Be Quick! Bring Packs!," p. 291; Kuhlman, *Legend into History,* p. 101; *Abstract,* p. 180 (Godfrey).

41. *Abstract,* pp. 141, 148 (Benteen), 26 (Wallace), 108–9 (DeRudio); Graham, *Story of the Little Big Horn,* pp. 72–73.

42. Graham, *Story of the Little Big Horn,* p. 91; Stewart, *Custer's Luck,* p. 431; but see Robert J. Ege, *Curse Not His Curls,* pp. 120–132. The possibility of a survivor, however, does not materially alter our knowledge of the Last Stand.

43. Charles Kuhlman, *Gen. George A. Custer,* p.11; Kuhlman, *Legend into History,* p. 154.

44. Graham, "Come On! Be Quick! Bring Packs!," p. 289; Kuhlman, *Legend into History,* p. 154.

45. *Abstract,* pp. 136 (Benteen), 176 (Godfrey); Kuhlman, *Legend into History,* pp. 157–60; Graham, *Story of the Little Big Horn,* pp. 84–85; Stewart, *Custer's Luck,* pp. 338–39.

46. Graham, "Come On! Be Quick! Bring Packs!," p. 290; Kuhlman, *Legend into History,* pp. 159–62; Stewart, *Custer's Luck,* pp. 434–40. Whether or not—and, if so, how far—Custer led his five troops down the coulee toward the river is a disputed question. I tend to follow Stewart in this matter, chiefly because of his careful analysis of the terrain and circumstances, but partly also because of his psychological argument: "to ride away from a fight was not in keeping with the Custer character or disposition. It is almost inconceivable that he, believing, as he did, that attack and victory were practically synonymous terms, would execute [some other maneuver]" (p. 440). Kuhlman, among those disagreeing on this point, appears perfectly sound in his reconstruction of the way in which instructions were given to Trumpeter Martin *(Legend into History,* pp. 162–63).

47. Graham, *Story of the Little Big Horn,* p. 55; Stewart, *Custer's Luck,* p. 438.

48. George B. Grinnell, *The Fighting Cheyenne* (New York: Scribner's, 1915) p. 340; Graham, *Story of the Little Big Horn,* p. 87; Stewart, *Custer's Luck,* pp. 400, 449.

49. Stewart, *Custer's Luck,* pp. 449–50.

50. Ibid., pp. 455–56.

51. Ibid.

CHAPTER FIVE

1. Hughes, "Campaign against the Sioux," pp. 32–33.

2. Ibid., p. 33.

3. *Centennial Campaign,* p. 357.

CHAPTER SIX

1. The origin of the Custer family has been disputed. For example, Merington, *Custer Story,* writes: "The Custers were of English origin, descended from the Cusiters of the Orkney Islands" (p. 3). However, Jay Monaghan, author of *Custer* and consultant to the Wyles Collection of Western

Americana, University of California, Santa Barbara, has informed me that a genealogy prepared by members of the Custer family and housed in the Wyles Collection indicates that the line goes back to one Paul Küster, born in 1630 in Hesse. The Germanic origin of the family is also confirmed by Lawrence A. Frost of Monroe, Michigan, author of several books on Custer, a friend of the Custer family, and probably the greatest living authority on matters pertaining to Custer's personal history. The reference to Emanuel Custer's fortunes is from Frost, *Custer Album*, pp. 17–18, and personal communication from Frost.

2. For the biographical data, see Frost, *Custer Album*, p. 18; Monaghan, *Custer*, p. 4. The births and deaths of the two sons is indicated in the Wyles Collection genealogy.

3. Frost, *Custer Album*, p. 18 and personal communication; Monaghan, *Custer*, pp. 4–5.

4. Monaghan, *Custer*, p. 3; Van de Water, *Glory-Hunter*, p. 22.

5. Monaghan, *Custer*, pp. 4–5, 261–62.

6. Ibid., p. 9; Van de Water, *Glory-Hunter*, p. 22; Frost, personal communication.

7. Monaghan, *Custer*, p. 5; Frost, personal communication.

8. Monaghan, *Custer*, p. 4; Frost, personal communication.

9. Elizabeth B. Custer, *''Boots and Saddles''*, p. 75. Libbie Custer's memoirs of her married life, while naturally biased, are a valuable source of colorful and revealing anecdotes.

10. Elizabeth B. Custer, *Tenting on the Plains*, 2:287–88. Libbie quotes verbatim from Emanuel Custer, though in the original the old man wrote ''Michigan'' instead of ''Ohio,'' an obvious slip of the pen. See Monaghan, *Custer*, p. 3.

11. Van de Water, *Glory-Hunter*, p. 22.

12. Ibid., pp. 23–24; Frost, personal communication.

13. The movements of various members of the Custer family between southeastern Ohio and the Monroe area were rather complex and occupied some fifteen years, roughly from 1842 to 1858. The basic data are contained in Frost, *General Custer's Libbie*, pp. 44–45; Monaghan, *Custer*, pp. 6–12.

14. Monaghan, *Custer*, pp. 7–8.

15. Frost, *Custer Album*, pp. 19–20; Van de Water, *Glory-Hunter*, p. 24.

16. Quoted in George Armstrong Custer, *My Life on the Plains*, ed. Milo M. Quaife (Chicago: Lakeside Press; R. R. Donnelly Co., 1952), p. xxiv.

17. *Custer*, p. 8.

18. Ibid., pp. 8–9.

19. References to Custer's strong physique and athleticism may be found in almost all of the biographical works and in Libbie Custer's three memoirs. The fear of water is mentioned in Van de Water, *Glory-Hunter*, p. 23.

20. For Custer's schooling, see Frost, *General Custer's Libbie*, pp. 44–45; the letter to Bingham is quoted in Van de Water, *Glory-Hunter*, p. 26; the sale of the Custer farm is mentioned in Monaghan, *Custer*, p. 12, and confirmed by Frost, personal communication.

21. Monaghan, *Custer*, p. 42.

22. Ibid., pp. 20, 30.

CHAPTER SEVEN

1. Whittaker, *Complete Life*, pp. 51–52.

2. Monaghan, *Custer*, pp. 49–56; Van de Water, *Glory-Hunter*, p. 37.

3. Monaghan, *Custer*, pp. 57–58; Whittaker, *Complete Life*, p. 83.

4. Frost, *Custer Album*, p. 28.

5. Ibid., p. 30.

6. *Custer*, p. 74.

7. George B. McClellan, *McClellan's Own Story* (New York: Charles L. Webster and Co., 1887), p. 123; Frost, *Custer Album*, p. 33.

8. Frost, *Custer Album*, p. 33.

9. *Complete Life*, p. 9.

10. Ibid., pp. 161–62. Custer's commission as brevet brigadier general is held at the Custer Battlefield National Monument.

11. Charles D. Rhodes, *History of the Cavalry of the Army of the Potomac* (Kansas City, Mo.: Hudson, 1900), p. 67.

12. William E. Miller, ''The Cavalry Battle near Gettysburg,'' in *Battles and Leaders of the Civil War*, 3 vols. (New York: Century, 1884), 3:397–406.

13. Frost, *Custer Album*, pp. 41–42; Monaghan, *Custer*, pp. 162–63.

14. For Sheridan's recognition of Custer's combat ability, see Frost, *Custer Album*, p. 42; Custer's being given command of the Third Cavalry Division is noted in *Official Records, War of the Rebellion*, vol. 43, pt. 2, p. 218 (National Archives). Custer's various titles can be confusing. Along with many other officers, he held three types of commissions: in the Regular Army; of temporary rank (for example, as an aide or in the volunteer forces); and brevet commissions, issued in recognition of especially meritorious service. Brevet commissions carried no implications with respect to either command or pay; they were honorary titles. It was the custom, however, to use such titles in informally addressing the officer so designated, whatever his rank might currently be in the Regular Army. Thus Custer was addressed for the rest of his life as "General," except in formal military communications, and thus he would address both Major Reno and Captain Benteen as "Colonel."

The following is a list of the commissions and the dates they were granted possessed by Custer at the time of his death. The actual documents are now in the museum of the Custer Battlefield National Monument.

24 June 1861	second lieutenant, Second Regiment of Cavalry
5 June 1862	additional aide-de-camp, with the rank of captain
29 June 1863	brigadier general of volunteers
3 July 1863	brevet major, for gallant and meritorious services at the battle of Gettysburg, Pennsylvania
17 July 1863	first lieutenant, Fifth Regiment of Cavalry
8 May 1864	captain, Fifth Regiment of Cavalry
11 May 1864	brevet lieutenant colonel, for gallant and meritorious services at the battle of Yellow Tavern, Virginia
19 Sept. 1864	brevet colonel, for gallant and meritorious services at the battle of Winchester, Virginia
13 Mar. 1865	brevet brigadier general, for gallant and meritorious services at the battle of Five Forks, Virginia
13 Mar. 1865	brevet major general, for gallant and meritorious services during the campaign ending with the surrender of the insurgent Army of Northern Virginia
15 Apr. 1865	major general of volunteers
28 July 1866	lieutenant colonel, Seventh Regiment of Cavalry

15. Monaghan, *Custer*, pp. 240–42.

16. The original letter is in the Elizabeth B. Custer Collection, Custer Battlefield National Monument, now on permanent loan to the Eastern Montana University Library. For Custer's military action preceding Lee's surrender, see John Gibbon, "Personal Recollections of Appomattox," *Century Illustrated Monthly Magazine* 53 (April 1902):938–40.

CHAPTER EIGHT

1. Monaghan, *Custer*, pp. 264–65; Frost, *Custer Album*, p. 72.
2. Whittaker, *Complete Life*, pp. 339–41.
3. Monaghan, *Custer*, p. 269.
4. Monaghan, *Custer*, pp. 269–79.
5. Ibid., pp. 281–82; Merington, *Custer Story*, p. 211.
6. Monaghan, *Custer*, p. 282.
7. Ibid., p. 284; Van de Water, *Glory-Hunter*, pp. 151–52.
8. Monaghan, *Custer*, p. 285; Lawrence A. Frost, *The Court-Martial of General George Armstrong Custer*, pp. 37–49. The latter book contains a careful abstract of the court-martial proceedings and much verbatim material.
9. George A. Custer, *My Life on the Plains*, p. 66; Frost, *Court-Martial*, pp. 53–54.
10. Monaghan, *Custer*, pp. 293–94.
11. Ibid., pp. 294–95; E. Custer, *Tenting on the Plains*, 3:670.

12. Monaghan, *Custer,* pp. 295–96; Frost, *Court-Martial,* pp. 69–71, 166–70 (testimony of Acting Assistant Surgeon I. T. Coates).

13. Monaghan, *Custer,* p. 297.

14. Frost, *Court-Martial,* p. 81.

15. Monaghan, *Custer,* p. 299; G. Custer, *My Life on the Plains,* p. 117. Custer gives the time as fifty-five hours, but he seems to have meant marching time.

16. G. Custer, *My Life on the Plains,* p. 118; Frost, *Court-Martial,* pp. 85–86; Monaghan, *Custer,* pp. 299–300.

17. Frost, *Court-Martial,* pp. 88–89; Frost, personal communication.

18. Frost, *Court-Martial,* pp. 96, 99–102.

19. Ibid., pp. 198–99. This point is interesting because it suggests that Elliott had developed considerable personal loyalty to Custer by this time.

20. Ibid., pp. 245–47, a literal transcription from the original proceedings, made available to Frost by the Judge Advocate General, Department of the Army.

21. G. Custer, *My Life on the Plains,* p. xv.

22. Frost, *Court-Martial,* p. 256; the original is in Frost's collection.

23. G. Custer, *My Life on the Plains,* p. 183; the original is in the William J. Ghent Papers, Library of Congress.

24. Merington, *Custer Story,* p. 217.

25. G. Custer, *My Life on the Plains,* p. 184; Monaghan, *Custer,* p. 306.

26. G. Custer, *My Life on the Plains,* p. 210.

27. Ibid., pp. 214–24.

28. Ibid., pp. 229–33. The tragic irony of the crying infant was not lost on Custer, who commented on it (p. 233).

29. Ibid., p. 234; Monaghan, *Custer,* pp. 316–17.

30. Monaghan, *Custer,* pp. 317–18.

31. Ibid., p. 320.

32. Ibid.; G. Custer, *My Life on the Plains,* pp. 247–59.

33. G. Custer, *My Life on the Plains,* pp. 266–68.

34. Reprinted in the *New York Times,* 14 February 1869.

35. Monaghan, *Custer,* p. 320.

36. Elizabeth B. Custer, *Following the Guidon,* p. 246, for Custer's application for West Point; for the leaves of absence and the Elizabethtown assignment, see Monaghan, *Custer,* pp. 332–35.

37. Monaghan, *Custer,* pp. 338–39; Frost, *Custer Album,* p. 109.

38. For Custer's attitude toward Stanley's drinking, see Frost, *Custer Album,* p. 112; for Custer's arrest, see Monaghan, *Custer,* pp. 342–43.

39. Jackson, *Custer's Gold,* pp. 1–34; Monaghan, *Custer,* pp. 353–54. Jackson's volume is the definitive account of the Black Hills expedition of 1874.

40. Jackson, *Custer's Gold,* pp. 101–2 and map preceding p. 1.

41. Ibid., pp. 81–85.

42. Quoted ibid., pp. 87–88.

43. Quoted ibid., p. 89.

CHAPTER NINE

1. *Tenting on the Plains,* 3:621. Libbie's having regarded herself as a tomboy is a family tradition communicated to me by Frost.

2. Ibid., p. 536.

3. *Following the Guidon,* p. 66.

4. Custer family tradition communicated by Frost.

5. Merington, *Custer Story,* p. 121.

6. P. 86.

7. Merington, *Custer Story,* p. 105.

8. Ibid., p. 112.

9. *''Boots and Saddles'',* p. 102.

10. Quoted, with background material, in Frost, *General Custer's Libbie,* p. 163; the original is in the private Col. Brice C. W. Custer Collection. I do not intend to imply that Custer and Libbie did not

have a satisfactory sexual adjustment; what evidence there is suggests that they probably did. Libbie was devoted and irrepressible. For example, in an undated letter to Custer from Elizabethtown, Kentucky, she concluded, "now it is solitude itself—but with you here it will seem sunshiny and bright. Your loving bunkey i.e., bunk-mate, Libbie" (Elizabeth C. Custer Collection, Custer Battlefield Museum). As for Custer himself, the sense of this work is not that his neurotic conflicts were extraordinarily great, but that they were specific, largely identifiable, and related to events at the Little Big Horn (see chap. 10).

11. Merington, *Custer Story,* pp. 115, 122; Jackson, *Custer's Gold,* p. 97.

12. Merington, *Custer Story,* pp. 307–8.

13. Ibid., p. 142; Monaghan, *Custer,* p. 342; Jackson, *Custer's Gold,* p. 98.

14. *Tenting on the Plains,* 2:388–89.

15. Ibid., 3:544.

16. Ibid., pp. 563, 571.

17. Ibid., pp. 582–83.

18. Frost, *Custer Album,* p. 106.

19. *"Boots and Saddles",* pp. 5, 31–32.

20. *Tenting on the Plains,* 3:615.

21. E. Custer, *Following the Guidon,* p. 122; E. Custer, *"Boots and Saddles",* p. 23. The liking for pets seems to have been primarily Custer's, though Libbie was generally tolerant of them (Frost, personal communication).

22. *Following the Guidon,* p. 81. For Libbie's resistance to adoption, see Frost, *General Custer's Libbie,* p. 177.

23. *General Custer's Libbie,* p. 177. In a personal communication Frost told me that old-time cavalrymen commonly believed that the heat and trauma to the testes and perineum resulting from long days in the saddle could cause sterility; urologist colleagues of mine feel unable either to confirm or refute this, but the belief itself could be significant. Sandoz's claim is discussed by Monaghan, *Custer,* p. 328, to whom she made available her notes on the subject. The Fort Sill medical records for 1868 and 1869, earlier presumed lost, were reexamined in 1977 by D. E. Beckman, M.D., and found to contain no evidence that either George Armstrong or Tom Custer was treated for venereal disease ("Did Custer Have Syphilis?" *Little Big Horn Associates' Research Review* 11, no. 9 (1977):15–17. Sandoz in general reveals an anti-Custer bias, no doubt related to her sympathy for the Plains Indians, many of whom she knew well; it is possible that she was relying on hearsay. She may also simply have been confused as to dates or place. Custer's medical records are incomplete, and one cannot be certain.

24. Sandoz's views on the relationship between Custer and Mo-nah-se-tah are expressed in various places, notably in *Cheyenne Autumn,* p. 16. As Monaghan has shown, the dates of Mo-nah-se-tah's being taken into camp and of the birth make it impossible for Custer to have fathered the child, though he does note Benteen's reference to cuckoldry (*Custer,* pp. 327–28).

CHAPTER TEN

1. Cyrus Townsend Brady, "War with the Sioux," *Pearson's Magazine* 12 (1904):171.

2. *My Life on the Plains,* p. 22. The words "I often think" were not used in the original *Galaxy* article from which Custer took this passage. Custer was not a fanatic, despite various recent portrayals, and he often saw much to admire in his military opponents. For example, many of his friendships with former West Point classmates who fought on the Confederate side survived the Civil War.

3. Van de Water, *Glory-Hunter,* p. 229.

4. *Character Analysis,* trans. Theodore P. Wolfe, 3d ed. (New York: Orgone Institute Press, 1949), pp. 200–207.

5. Heinz Kohut, "Forms and Transformations of Narcissism," *Journal of the American Psychoanalytic Association* 14 (1966):243–72; Heinz Kohut and Philip F. D. Seitz, "Concepts and Theories of Psychoanalysis," in J. M. Wepman and R. W. Hein, eds., *Concepts of Personality* (Chicago: Aldine, 1963), pp. 113–41; Paul H. Ornstein, "Trends in Psychoanalysis," *Ohio State Medical Journal* 64 (1968):53–57.

6. Anna Freud, *The Ego and Mechanisms of Defense* (New York: International Universities Press, 1946), p. 51.

7. George B. Herendeen in *New York Herald Tribune,* 22 January 1878, p. 4; "I was standing on the forward deck of the [*Far West*] when I was called into the cabin where I found Generals Terry,

Gibbon, Custer and Brisbin around a table apparently holding a council of war. Terry showed me a map and asked me for information about the country on Tulloch's Fork and Little Big Horn. I understood from the conversation had by Terry with Gibbon and Custer that he was trying to find out where the columns of Custer and Gibbon could best form a juncture, somewhere in the neighborhood of the mouth of the Little Big Horn, Custer to march up the Rosebud and Gibbon up the Big Horn. I had been over the ground and told the General all about it."

8. Stewart, *Custer's Luck,* p. 319.

9. Edgerly, Weir's lieutenant at the Battle of the Little Big Horn, wrote this, with the indicated emphasis, to W. A. Graham, who quoted it in *Custer Myth,* p. 217.

Bibliography

Andrist, Ralph K. *The Long Death*. New York: Collier Books, 1964.

Bailey, John W. *Pacifying the Plains: General Alfred Terry and the Decline of the Sioux, 1866–1890*. Westport, Conn.: Greenwood Press, 1979.

Beckman, D. E. "Did Custer Have Syphilis?" *Little Big Horn Associates' Research Review* 11 (1977):15–17.

Benteen, Frederick W. "An Account of the Little Big Horn Campaign." Typed transcript in William J. Ghent Papers, Library of Congress, Washington, D.C.

Bourke, John G. *On the Border with Crook*. New York: Charles Scribner's Sons, 1891. Reprinted Lincoln, Nebr.: University of Nebraska Press, 1971.

Bradley, James H. *The March of the Montana Column*. Edited by Edgar I. Stewart. Norman, Okla.: University of Oklahoma Press, 1961.

Brady, Cyrus Townsend. *Indian Fights and Fighters*. Garden City, N.Y.: Doubleday, Page and Co., 1904. Reprinted with an introduction by James T. King, Lincoln, Nebr.: University of Nebraska Press, 1971.

Brill, Charles J. *Conquest of the Southern Plains*. Oklahoma City, Okla.: Golden Saga Publishers, 1938.

Brininstool, Earl A. *Troopers with Custer*. Harrisburg, Pa.: Stackpole Co., 1952. Rev. and expanded ed. of *A Trooper with Custer*, Columbus, Ohio: Trader-Trapper Co., 1925.

Camp, Walter. *Walter Camp's Notes on the Custer Fight*. Edited by Kenneth Hammer. Provo, Utah: Brigham Young University Press, 1976.

Carroll, John M. *Custer in Periodicals*. Fort Collins, Colo.: Old Army Press, 1974.

———. *Four on Custer by Carroll*. New Brunswick, N.J.: Guidon Press, 1976.

———, ed. *The Papers of the Order of Indian Wars*. Fort Collins, Colo.: Old Army Press, 1975.

———, and Price, Byron. *Roll Call on the Little Big Horn, 28 June 1876*. Fort Collins, Colo.: Old Army Press, 1975.

Custer, Elizabeth B. *"Boots and Saddles"*. New York: Harper and Bros., 1885. Reprinted with an introduction by Jane R. Stewart, Norman, Okla.: University of Oklahoma Press, 1961.

———. *Following the Guidon*. New ed. with an introduction by Jane R. Stewart. Norman, Okla.: University of Oklahoma Press, 1966. Original ed. New York: Harper and Bros., 1890.

———. *Tenting on the Plains*. New ed. with an introduction by Jane R. Stewart. 3 vols. Norman, Okla.: University of Oklahoma Press, 1971. Original ed. New York: Charles L. Webster and Co., 1887.

Custer, George A. *My Life on the Plains*. New ed. with an introduction by Edgar I. Stewart. Norman, Okla.: University of Oklahoma Press, 1962. Original ed. New York: Sheldon and Co., 1874.

Dippie, Brian W. *Custer's Last Stand: The Anatomy of an American Myth*. Missoula, Mont.: University of Montana Press, 1976.

Du Mont, John S. *Custer Battle Guns*. Fort Collins, Colo.: Old Army Press, 1974.

Dustin, Fred. *The Custer Fight*. Hollywood, Calif.: privately printed, 1936.

———. *The Custer Tragedy*. Ann Arbor, Mich.: Edwards Bros., 1939.

Edgerly, Winfield S. "Narrative of the March of General George A. Custer." Typed transcription in William J. Ghent Papers, Library of Congress, Washington, D.C.

Ege, Robert J. *Curse Not His Curls*. Fort Collins, Colo.: Old Army Press, 1974.

Frost, Lawrence A. *The Court-Martial of General George Armstrong Custer*. Norman, Okla.: University of Oklahoma Press, 1968.

———. *The Custer Album*. Seattle, Wash.: Superior Publishing Co., 1964.

———. *General Custer's Libbie*. Seattle, Wash.: Superior Publishing Co., 1976.

Gibbon, John. "Last Summer's Expedition against the Sioux and Its Great Catastrophe." *American Catholic Quarterly Review* 2 (April, 1877):271–304.

Godfrey, Edward S. "Custer's Last Battle." *Century Illustrated Monthly Magazine* 43 (January 1892):358–87.

———. "Custer's Last Battle." *Contributions to the Historical Society of Montana* 9 (1923):141–225.

———. "Diary of Captain E. S. Godfrey, Battle of the Little Big Horn, 1876." Part 1 among William J. Ghent Papers; Part 2 among Edward S. Godfrey MSS, both in Library of Congress, Washington, D.C.

Graham, W. A. "Come On! Be Quick! Bring Packs!" *Cavalry Journal* 32 (July 1923):303–17.

———. *The Custer Myth: A Source Book of Custeriana*. Harrisburg, Pa.: Stackpole Co., 1953.

———. *The Reno Court of Inquiry*. Pacific Palisades, Calif.: privately printed, 1951. Reprinted Harrisburg, Pa.: Stackpole Co., 1954.

———. *The Story of the Little Big Horn*. New York: Century, 1926.

Gray, John S. *Centennial Campaign: The Sioux War of 1876*. Fort Collins, Colo.: Old Army Press, 1976.

Hofling, Charles K. "General Custer and the Battle of the Little Big Horn." *Psychoanalytic Review* 54 (Summer 1967):303–28. Reprinted in *Montana: The Magazine of Western History* 21 (1971):32–43.

Hughes, Robert P. "The Campaign against the Sioux in 1876." *Journal of the Military Service Institution of the United States* 18 (January 1896):1–44. Reprinted in W. A. Graham, *The Story of the Little Big Horn*.

Hutton, Paul A., ed. *Garry Owen 1976: Annual of the Little Big Horn Associates*. Seattle, Wash.: Little Big Horn Associates, 1977.

Jackson, Donald. *Custer's Gold*. New Haven, Conn.: Yale University Press, 1966. Reprinted Lincoln, Nebr.: University of Nebraska Press, 1972.

Kanipe, Daniel A. "A New Story of Custer's Last Battle: Told by the Messenger Boy Who Survived." *Contributions to the Historical Society of Montana* 4 (1923):213–25.

Kaufman, Fred S. *Custer Passed Our Way*. Aberdeen, S. Dak.: North Plains Press, 1971.

Kinsley, D. A. *Favor the Bold*. 2 vols. New York: Holt, Rinehart and Winston, 1967, 1968.

Kohut, Heinz. "Forms and Transformations of Narcissism." *Journal of the American Psychoanalytic Association* 14 (1966): 243–72.

——— and Seitz, Philip F. D. "Concepts and Theories of Psychoanalysis," In J. M. Wepman and R. W. Hein, eds. *Concepts of Personality* (Chicago: Aldine, 1963), pp. 113–41.

Kuhlman, Charles. *General George A. Custer: A Lost Trail and the Gall Saga*. Billings, Mont.: privately printed, 1940.

———. *Legend into History*. Harrisburg, Pa.: Stackpole Co., 1952.

Liddic, Bruce L., ed. *I Buried Custer: The Diary of Pvt. Thomas W. Coleman, Seventh U.S. Cavalry*. College Station, Texas: Creative Publishing Co., 1979.

Luce, Edward S. *Keogh, Commanche, and Custer*. Saint Louis, Mo.: John S. Swift Co., 1939.

McClernand, Edward J. "With the Indian and the Buffalo in Montana." *Cavalry Journal* 36 (Jan.–April 1927):7–54.

McLaughlin, James. *My Friend the Indian*. New ed. with a preface by L. L. Pfaller. Seattle, Wash.: Superior Publishing Co., 1970. Original ed. New York: Houghton Mifflin Co., 1910.

Marquis, Thomas B. *Custer on the Little Big Horn*. Lodi, Calif.: End-Kian Publishing Co., 1967.

———. ed. and interp. *Wooden Leg: A Warrior Who Fought Custer*. Lincoln, Nebr.: University of Nebraska Press. Originally published as *A Warrior Who Fought Custer* (Midwest Co., 1931).

———. *Custer, Cavalry, and Crows*. Edited by John Popovich. Fort Collins, Colo.: Old Army Press, 1975.

Merington, Marguerite. *The Custer Story*. New York: Devin-Adair Co., 1950.

Miles, Nelson A. *Personal Recollections of General Nelson A. Miles*. Chicago: Werner Co., 1897.

Monaghan, Jay. *Custer: The Life of General George Armstrong Custer*. Lincoln, Nebr.: University of Nebraska Press, 1971.

Ornstein, Paul. "Trends in Psychoanalysis." *Ohio State Medical Journal* 64 (1968): 53–57.

Red Fox, William. *The Memoirs of Chief Red Fox*. New York: McGraw-Hill, 1971.

Reedstrom, Ernest Lisle. *Bugles, Banners, and War Bonnets*. Caldwell, Idaho: Caxton Printers, 1977.

Rosenberg, Bruce A. *Custer and the Epic of Defeat*. University Park, Pa.: Pennsylvania State University Press, 1974.

Sandoz, Mari. *The Battle of the Little Bighorn*. Philadelphia, Pa.: J.B. Lippincott Co., 1966.

———. *Cheyenne Autumn*. New York: Avon Books, 1953.

———. *Crazy Horse: The Strange Man of the Oglalas*. Lincoln, Nebr.: University of Nebraska Press, 1961. Original ed. New York: Hastings House, 1942.

Sheridan, Philip H. *Personal Memoirs of P. H. Sheridan*. 2 vols. New York: Charles L. Webster and Co., 1888.

Stewart, Edgar I. *Custer's Luck*. Norman, Okla.: University of Oklahoma Press, 1955.

———. "The Little Big Horn: 90 Years Later." *Montana: The Magazine of Western History* 16 (Spring 1966):2–13.

Taylor, Joseph Henry. "Bloody Knife and Gall." *North Dakota Historical Journal* 4 (July 1947):163–73.

Upton, Richard. *The Custer Adventure*. Fort Collins, Colo.: Old Army Press, 1975.

Utley, Robert M. *Custer Battlefield*. Historical Handbook Series No. 1. Washington, D.C.: Office of Publications, National Park Service, U.S. Department of the Interior, 1969.

———. *Custer and the Great Controversy*. Los Angeles, Calif.: Westernlore Press, 1962.

———. *The Reno Court of Inquiry*. Fort Collins, Colo.: Old Army Press, 1972.

Van de Water, Frederick F. *Glory-Hunter: A Life of General Custer*. Indianapolis, Ind.: Bobbs-Merrill, 1934.

Vaughn, J. W. *Indian Fights*. Norman, Okla.: University of Oklahoma Press, 1966.

Ware, Eugene F. *The Indian War of 1864*. New ed. with an introduction by Clyde C. Walton. New York: St. Martin's Press, 1960. Original ed. Topeka, Kans.: Crane and Co., 1911.

Whittaker, Frederick. *A Complete Life of Gen. George A. Custer*. New York: Sheldon and Co., 1876.

Index

A native of Ohio, Charles K. Hofling was educated at the University of Cincinnati College of Arts and Sciences, the University of Pennsylvania College of Medicine, and the University of Cincinnati College of Medicine, from which he received the M.D. degree in 1946. He received his psychiatric training at the Cincinnati General Hospital and the Menninger Foundation. Dr. Hofling served as associate professor of psychiatry at the University of Cincinnati College of Medicine, and later as professor of psychiatry at Saint Louis University and as a member of the faculty of the Graduate School, Saint Louis University. In addition, he belonged to several psychiatric, literary, and historical organizations.

Dr. Hofling published extensively on both medical-psychiatric and literary-historical topics. He was actively interested in the fields of western Americana and psychohistory, serving as chairman of the Task force on Psychohistory of the American Psychiatric Association from 1973 to 1976. This volume is his only full-length psychohistorical study.

The manuscript was edited by Sherwyn T. Carr. The book was designed by Edgar Frank. The typeface for the text is Times Roman, based on a design by Stanley Morrison. The display face is Melior, designed by Hermann Zapf about 1952.

The text is printed on International Paper Company's Bookmark natural text paper and the book is bound in Holliston Mills' Payko cloth over binder's boards. Manufactured in the United States of America.